Imagine That

JoJo Watts

Copyright © 2018 JoJo Watts

All rights reserved. No part(s) of this book may be reproduced, distributed or transmitted in any form, or by any means, or stored in a database or retrieval systems without prior expressed written permission of the author of this book.

ISBN: 978-1-5356-1236-4

Dedication

For Taylor, my loving husband, who has allowed me to stand beside him, hand in hand, as he loves me unconditionally with love and equality. And our beloved kids, Hunter, Mayor, and Wyatt.

Acknowledgments

Jennifer Campbell, who first gave this story life. Without judgment, she allowed me to be vulnerable. Her honesty and humorous opinions are most valuable and I am truly grateful. I will cherish our friendship forever.

Summer Forrest, your inspiration and encouragement will forever live with me. Thank you for reawakening my trust in me.

Mai Watts, Peter Lacoux, and Kiondra Henderson, for your daily support.

Hunter Watts, for your love, help, ideas, and constant support.

Wyatt and Mayor Watts, for your love and support.

Mom, Dad, and Grandmother for your unconditional love, values, grace, and never-ending support.

Contents

Chapter 1 1
Chapter 2 11
Chapter 3 15
Chapter 4 23
Chapter 5 35
Chapter 6 44
Chapter 7 52
Chapter 8 64
Chapter 9 84
Chapter 10 94
Chapter 11 104
Chapter 12 115
Chapter 13 124

Chapter 1

(August 1991)

It was early August, on a beautiful summer night in New York City. Singing to the tunes of John Mellencamp's "Jack & Diane," I danced to the door to greet my girlfriend Christine. As she walked in, we simultaneously sang together, "Change will come around real soon, make you women and men!" Ba da bop!! We were loud and jamming, feeling every bit of our twenty-three-year-old selves on a Thursday night in NYC. Christine arrived with an armload of our favorite snacks (chocolate-chip cookies and cookie-dough ice cream) and palpable excitement for me, as I was packing for a morning flight to Paris. Neither Christine nor I had ever traveled outside of the USA. As I packed, snacked, and sang, I thought to myself, How lucky am I to be having this opportunity?

Our mutual friend Eleanor and I were to be traveling with her boyfriend, Jack, to Paris for his business trip. I didn't know what he did for work, but it seemed important.

Weeks earlier, I'd met up for cocktails with Eleanor and Jack. At some point during the night, the conversation turned to Jack's near-future plans to travel to Paris.

"Wouldn't you prefer to have some company?" hinted Eleanor.

"You know I would...but I have so many appointments and obligations. You would be alone all day, and some evenings, too," said Jack, looking guilty.

"Well...what if Brooke and I both joined you? We could go sightseeing during the day and meet up with you when possible," suggested Eleanor.

Suddenly, Jack's entire demeanor changed. "That's actually a great idea, Eleanor!"

"Wait, what? I have no money to go to Paris! I don't even have money for sightseeing!" I interjected.

What the hell was Eleanor thinking?

"Listen," said Jack, "I think this would be fun for you gals. What if I took care of the flights? My company has an apartment on the left bank in Paris, and it's big enough for the three of us, so lodging is a done deal. Could you come up with money for food, Brooke?"

I was shocked to feel my head nodding yes while my mind was screaming "NOOOOO!" Food in Paris? I didn't even think I could afford to take off work for ten days. And would my boss allow that?

I took a deep breath, giving myself a reality check. "Until I talk with Nina, I can't even begin to consider your invitation."

Imagine That!

I was working as a freelancer in retail for cosmetics and fragrances while auditioning with the hopes of eventually landing my dream acting job. Nina was a great boss, an incredible woman that I admired. She was her family's primary breadwinner, while her husband took on odd jobs. Working as a freelancer allowed me flexibility, but Nina had hired me as a steady freelancer in Bloomingdales. I continued to work jobs at Saks Fifth Ave., Bergdorf Goodman, and Henri Bendel's. These high-end department stores in Manhattan attracted clients from all over the world. My job was fun and full of beautiful, diverse people, speaking the languages of many cultures.

I couldn't sleep at all that night. Restless dreams of Paris intermingled with my nervousness at approaching Nina.

Nina arrived late to work the next morning, and her mood was frantic and discombobulated. I had only one thing on my mind, and that was to figure out the right time to approach Nina. Eventually mid-morning came and she seemed settled.

"Nina? Is there a time I could talk to you about an opportunity I have?" I spat out.

No-nonsense Nina said, "Let's talk now. Are you taking another job?"

"No. No!" I stuttered. "I'm not leaving you or taking another job."

I continued at my usual rapid-fire pace to explain the possibility of a trip to Paris.

Her reaction was more than enthusiastic for me. "Brooke, that is an amazing opportunity, and yes, go!! I will get sufficient help." I couldn't call Eleanor fast enough!

Nina said go, Jack bought the tickets, I applied for a passport, and, fast-forward, Christine and I were packing my suitcase for Paris!

"Let's go out dancing!" exclaimed Christine.

At first I thought she was joking.

I was concentrating on my packing, all the while trying to figure out how I was going to afford food in Paris for ten days.

Christine and I both got a kick out of my travel arrangement, since we were always hungry and too broke to ever eat a sensible meal. This phenomenon was all too familiar with our group of friends – never any money, but always willing to have fun. I knew NYC was expensive, but I was easily living off pizza and dirty dogs at a dollar each, and unless I added toppings, I could usually eat for a week on ten dollars.

What I didn't know was the cost of food in Paris.

"Who cares?" said Christine. "You're going to fucking Paris! Let's go celebrate!"

Imagine That!

"Okay, okay!" I conceded.

Little did I know that night would change the course of my life.

Christine and I headed toward the Crane Club, an easy six blocks away from my apartment. This place was amazing on every level – it was an upscale, intimate setting with dining, dancing, and a small bar. We usually went on Thursday nights and mingled with the well-dressed people coming from a long workday. Arriving around midnight, we caught the attention of our bouncer friend Steve. Christine was infatuated with Steve, which worked to our advantage, as he nodded for us to enter without the customary twenty-dollar cover fee.

The Crane Club was hopping that night with loud music, high energy, and the NYC style I was adopting as my own. Christine made a beeline to the dance floor, while I lagged behind, pausing to survey the room. From the entrance area, I was soaking in the dancers and the people at the bar when my eye caught the attention of a tall, handsome guy sipping something while listening to one of the many people surrounding him. I averted my gaze and joined Christine on the dance floor as the song "O.P.P." by Naughty by Nature came on. We sang and danced ourselves into exhaustion listening to R.E.M., Nas, Counting Crows, Tupac, and Stone Temple Pilots.

Eventually, I ended up back at the entranceway to catch my breath.

Christine and I used the entranceway as our "meeting and resting spot" when not on the dance floor. It made it easy to keep track of one another. Neither of us were big drinkers; I did not enjoy the taste, nor did I have the money for such indulgence.

I continued to watch the dance floor. Suddenly, I was face to face with the tall, handsome guy from the bar.

"Hello," he said as he passed me on the way to the restrooms.

"Hi," I replied.

A few minutes later he returned, and as I was considering returning to the dance floor, I noticed he had stopped and was standing behind me. Moments later, I heard his polite voice. "What's your name? I'm Harrison." In my mind I hoped he was indeed talking to me…

"Brooke," I choked out.

"Nice to meet you. Do you live here, in the city?"

"I do," I managed.

This conversation was off and running as Harrison followed up with questions regarding my work, my friends, and my hometown.

"I can't believe you're from Springdale." He smiled. "I was just there! A good friend of mine from college, Michael, just married a girl from Springdale."

Imagine That!

"What's her name?" I asked. "I know everyone in Springdale."

Surprisingly, I did know Leah! What a small world!

Harrison was so easy to talk to, and as we continued chatting, we moved over to a bench in the foyer. I learned that he was living in New Jersey with a friend, and he was here at the club with about fifteen college friends. He was smooth, funny, and he seemed very smart. He appeared to be worldly for someone in his mid-twenties and spoke of places in America I'd never even heard of before. (How the hell was I supposed to know where Martha's Vineyard was? I'd barely traveled outside of my home state!)

At some point, I asked Harrison if he'd like to dance. He nodded and followed me to the dance floor. We danced a little, but we kept trying to talk to one another over the music. Eventually giving up, we retreated back to the bench and continued our conversation. As the night was growing late, Harrison asked, "Brooke, can I see you again?"

"I would love that," I replied. "But I am leaving town for the next ten days." I launched into a shortened version of the previous week and my adventures in preparation for my trip to Paris.

"That's great!" exclaimed Harrison. "Will you go to the Louvre?"

"The what?" I asked. "The Louvre? What's that?" As soon as it came out of my mouth, I knew that I should have known what the Louvre was.

The look on his face was stunned, but so as to not embarrass me, he offered a follow-up question. "Do you know the painting the *Mona Lisa*?"

"Of course," I answered confidently.

"The Louvre is a museum that houses the *Mona Lisa*," he said.

"Oh," I said, feeling completely stupid, yet grateful that Harrison seemed to have protected my ego. "Have you been there?"

"Yes, I have," replied Harrison.

Holy shit, Handsome Harrison had been to Paris.

"Would you be willing to recommend some places that Eleanor and I may be interested in seeing?"

Harrison smiled. "Of course!"

Steve the bouncer gave me pencil and paper and I rushed back to write down all the locations that Harrison recommended: the Eiffel Tower (I did know that one!), the Palace of Versailles, Notre Dame, Champs-Élysées, and the Musée d'Orsay, the foreign-sounding words rolling easily from Harrison's mouth…

I snapped back to attention when I realized that one of Harrison's friends, who was equally impressive in size was making a second walk around our bench giving him the "what the hell?" eyes. They had clearly planned a guys' night out and I was clearly not a guy.

"I'm sorry, Harrison," I offered. "I think I may have taken too much of your time. Your friend does not seem happy."

"My friend will be fine, Brooke. Can I walk you home?"

We gathered Christine and walked back to my apartment building.

As we wished one another good night, Harrison asked for my phone number.

"I'll call you in ten days," he said.

Seriously?

Christine and I met back upstairs and she pummeled me with questions about "the big guy." I told her about my horrific embarrassment over the Louvre and Harrison's valiant attempt to rescue me. We laughed our asses off.

I was positive that Harrison would not be calling. However, I would go out with him if he did.

But no guy would call after such a lame impression and a ten-day wait…

NYC is so big that our experience with guys had been: if they didn't call you the next day, they weren't going to call. We didn't mind that anyway. So much life was going on in the city, and we were having the best time of our lives being broke, cute, and striving for big-city dreams.

Since we were from small towns, everything we did was considered the best ever. Christine left around 4:30 a.m. to go back to Hoboken, New Jersey, wishing me all the best that Paris had to offer and more. As I packed the last few items in my bag, I found myself thinking about him. He was a tall (six foot four), broad, athletically built, white guy. Blond hair framed his face, and the bluest of eyes that stared, with certainty unknown to me. He had a chiseled jawbone that complemented his steady demeanor. He walked with confidence that was smooth and measured with certitude. Definitely sexy in a discreet manner, and his sizable vocabulary was captivating. He truly seemed to be the smartest person I've met. Imagine that!

Chapter 2

Eleanor was listening to a tutorial on her Walkman, a beginner's guide to speaking French. As we sat on the tarmac waiting for the plane to leave, I stared out the window at the NYC skyline, asking myself, How the hell did I get here? I'm a very long way from the streets I once knew.

Growing up in a small town in Florida seemed like forever ago. I lived in a neighborhood with low-income affordable houses for families like mine, who didn't have the means to meet certain minimum qualifications. The homes were divided into neighborhoods, Old Projects, New Projects, and the Sable Palm Projects, and consisted of one- to four-bedroom duplex apartments.

When my parents divorced, my mother, brother, and I moved into the Old Projects, just down the street from my paternal grandparents. Years later, we moved into a three-bedroom apartment directly across the street from them. Surrounded by an abundance of family members, we never had money for anything extra. The neighbors were all hard-working folks trying to make a dollar out of fifteen cents. Asking for money was a chore – and the answer was always "NO!" My mother worked long hours, and my brother and I were latchkey kids, often home alone. Once, my mother forbade us to go outside when she left for work. We promptly disobeyed and began to play with the boy next door. The boys were throwing a baseball between the dividers of the houses and dared me to try to do the same. I took the dare, and accidentally threw the ball into neighbor's window, shattering the glass. The boys reported to the lady of the house, whom I knew very well, that it was me who broke the window. She told me to tell my mom and let her know the details of how her window would be repaired.

I was terrified and frightened beyond belief for many reasons! 1) I knew my mom didn't have the money to fix the window. 2) She would realize that I had disobeyed her orders to stay in the house. 3) She was going light my hide!

I nervously walked down the block to my grandmother's house. Three of my aunts and one uncle were there, and I begged them to give me money to fix the window before my mom got home. The house-wide consensus was, "Brooke, ain't nobody got no money for that!" I walked up and down the two long blocks of my street asking neighbors to help, but to no avail. "You must tell your mom," they kindly echoed.

Imagine That!

Those were the longest five hours of my life, waiting for Mom to come home from work. Finally, she drove up in her yellow Ford mustang, got out of the car carrying a bag of groceries, and I nervously spat out the details about the window. She dropped the bag of groceries, and, as I expected, gave me a whooping I would never, ever forget. As she was hitting me, she was accentuating every blow with a word: "We…have…no…extra…money…for…your…poor…judgments!"

I felt horrible. My mom didn't even like that neighbor, and now she had to fix her window with money we did not have.

It wasn't until my adolescent years that I started to notice the economic disparity between my family and my school friends. I would be invited to socialize in their homes – all lovely compared to mine – and their streets were quiet and empty. Where I lived, homes were crowded; kids were always outside, playing hopscotch and foursquare, jumping ropes, and riding bikes. The older boys would organize a pick-up basketball game, and huge crowds would gather to watch the next NBA hopeful.

By high school, I began to fantasize about how I would escape the circle of poverty surrounding me. I concentrated on activities like cheerleading and auditioning for the drama club. My drama teacher was very encouraging. "You have talent, Brooke. You should pursue this path."

I eventually started talking to my grandmother, an amazing and positive woman, about my dreams. "Brooke, there are ways you can have what you want in these times. Things are different for you than they were for me growing up."

She would continue to tell me about her childhood in Georgia, picking cotton, completing only an eighth-grade education, and marrying my grandfather at an early age. I loved her stories. Her main message was this: "We all start at one point in life, but can choose not to end up where we started."

"You dream big, Brooke," she said.

That's what I did. I dreamed.

Chapter 3

WE ARRIVED IN PARIS EARLY morning and were happy to start sightseeing. Our cab pulled up to the side of the road near a gate. As we got out, it looked empty. As we opened the door, it opened into a cobblestone road with many apartments. We notice Parisians opening their windows for fresh air. We found our apartment, and the place was more than big enough for three people. I too opened my bedroom window for fresh air and noticed immediately no screens, assuming no bugs. We quickly settled and decided to take the morning to rest up before taking to the sights and familiarizing ourselves with the neighborhood. I was determined to see everything that Harrison had recommended. On our first day of sightseeing, we learned that Eleanor's boyfriend, Jack, would not be joining us. Secretly, I was thrilled! We could concentrate on visiting these amazing places, without distraction, and, better yet, I didn't have to feel like a third wheel. First things first, the Louvre! It was a huge museum, packed with so many visitors and wonderful art. We walked for hours, searching for the famous painting, and once we found it, I stared at the beautiful Mona Lisa. She was surrounded by various groups of people – even American students on a school trip. As I listened to the students speaking English, their accent and speech patterns felt comforting.

We had also done some research on our own and read about a famous dance club. Music? Dancing? Yes, please! One night, Eleanor and I got dressed up and off we went. When we arrived at the club, we weren't feeling all that confident that we could get in. There was this big woman who stood out front, choosing the people that she thought fit to enter. We were fortunate that night (and yes, we did look cute) because she did choose us. The music was unique and the excitement high – we danced all night!

Then, once again, I went back to Harrison's list. We dined in a restaurant at the bottom of the Eiffel Tower. The beauty and history of Versailles was beyond my comprehension. Eleanor and I were kindly escorted by two friends we had met the night before. They both played professional football (soccer), and somehow persuaded us in allowing them to show us Versailles. We both had no idea on how massive it was. We walked forever, enjoying the manicured lawns, gorgeous flowers, and the sculptures that were fountains located throughout the gardens. Breathtaking were our emotions, so much so that we stopped to take many photos and found ourselves short of time to continue admiring this magnificent palace. We walked all over Paris, taking in the intoxicating architecture and culture. At one point, I began to notice similarities (like cobblestone streets) between Paris and SoHo, NY.

Our favorite past time was window shopping. I admired the Parisians; they were so friendly and helpful wherever we went. I'd walk into a shop, speaking English, and immediately the workers would stop doing what they were doing and greet us with delight, saying, "Bonjour, bonjour!"

And the elusive answer to the Million Dollar Question: "How does one afford to eat in Paris for ten days?" I ate baguettes with ham and cheese the entire trip, bought from street vendors. Therefore, I was able to afford my meals. One particular afternoon, about four days into our trip, Eleanor and I had been walking, and had just devoured a ham and cheese sandwich, when she and I came upon this adorable, quaint restaurant that seated about four tables. We decide that we would go in and have a glass of champagne. As we walked in, a couple was sitting near the opened windows to people watch. Not really paying attention, the woman said, "Brooke!" Matching her surprise, I said, "Caroline!" We had an exchange, back and forth, about why was I here in Paris. I told her the whole story. Caroline and Nina worked full-time, side by side, with one another in Bloomingdales. Caroline had eloped and was in Paris for her honeymoon. Eleanor and I sat with Caroline and her new husband for about an hour before moving on to our next adventure, to the Right Bank of Paris. As we walked across the bridge, I loved seeing the many artists lined up with their canvases, brushes, and paint, capturing the beautiful light of the romantic city. I was full of excitement!

Now that I had seen Paris and lived in New York, my goals were becoming clearer: I wanted more traveling. I enjoyed the people I'd met, and it left me with curiosity to see more. I knew that in order to pursue my dreams, I would need to make enough money to allow me to live a quality of life that included culture, style, and travel. This was not a model I'd grown up with – my family were hard-working people with jobs that paid the bills, but traveling was not something we did. Occasionally, we would take road trips to Georgia to visit my maternal great-grandma. We would leave about four a.m. and travel for nine hours and stay about four to five days. That was my entire travel history.

Living in NYC and working as a freelance model for fragrances and cosmetics might seem mindless, but it allowed me flexibility to audition for acting jobs. I was surrounded by the best in fashion, and my own style was changing. I didn't only wear nice clothes just because I was going to church; I looked and smelled good all the time! I learned all about fashion designers and how colors and patterns were put together. I learned what was chic, elegant, classic, or trendy, I learned how to purchase investment pieces, and I welcomed every bit of change that was happening.

Upon returning to my apartment from Paris, I called my mom to let her know that I was stateside and shared the trip with her. As I was speaking to her, I was receiving a call-waiting signal and asked Mom to hold. I clicked over to answer, and who should it be? The voice that I had secretly hoped (but never believed) would call – Harrison's! I told him I was talking to my mom and asked if I could call him back shortly; I wasn't confident that my mom knew of the places I was describing to her in Paris, anyway. I'm sure she was just relieved that I was back safely on American soil.

I immensely enjoyed calling Harrison back. I couldn't wait to tell him that the first thing Eleanor and I did was see the *Mona Lisa*! I shared with him a little more of the trip, but I tried not to talk so much. He was a gracious listener and asked all the right questions. And then, suddenly – "Would you like to go out on a date with me, Brooke?"

"Yes," I answered, a little too quickly.

We spoke once more, later in the week, to confirm our date. We agreed that lunch was best, as it would allow both of us to be at ease. Also, if I had to share the cost of the meal, I knew I would have the funds for a lunch date. I was so looking forward to sharing my trip with him, and a little part of me wanted to redeem my ego.

The night before our lunch date, I'd planned a dinner for Eleanor and Jack as a "thank you" for providing the opportunity of a lifetime for me. They chose a Japanese restaurant nearby. Of course, I'd never had Japanese food before, but since living in New York, I was always ready to experience new things.

The three of us dined and talked mostly about Paris. Jack was older than we were, and he schooled me on how to order from the menu. He described the difference between sushi and sashimi, the sauces and preparations, and gave me tips on using chopsticks. He ordered sake, and I drank that for the first time as we laughed and looked through all of our photos.

It turned out to be an early evening, and I was home by ten p.m., watching television in my pajamas.

Once I got comfortable, I started to feel sick. The kind of sick that makes your body react in ways you didn't think were possible…the kind of sick that has you, at twenty-three years old, calling out for your mama…the kind of sick that leaves you hunched over in pain. The kind of sick that has you helpless from eleven p.m. until eight a.m. the next morning…

Imagine That!

Harrison called around noon, and I began to tell him that I was not feeling well. He said, "I'm downstairs."

"What?" I said. "Okay. Give me fifteen minutes and I'll come right down."

I bolted into damage-control mode – I scrubbed my weak body and brushed my teeth and tongue profusely, trying to eliminate all traces of the stench of sickness. As I rapidly dressed, I convinced myself that, although not in a mood for entertaining, I was doing this. I managed a smile as I gathered the strength to walk down to greet Harrison. Thankfully, we didn't venture far and settled for a diner a block away. We ordered soup and a turkey sandwich as I prepared to impress him with my newfound knowledge of the Louvre and all the other places of Paris that he'd recommended.

But instead, I listened to him.

Harrison had just returned from visiting with his family on Martha's Vineyard. While he was there, the island was hit by Hurricane Bob. The island was devastated, and many were left without power. I shared with him that, growing up in Florida, we'd had many situations like that. He told me how the local authorities advised the residents to stay inside until further notice. As he and his family listened to the radio to receive information and storm status updates, a news anchor reported that one man was spotted down at the pier saying, "I've never missed a good storm yet, and I'm not going to now!" At that moment, a big wave swooshed in a wiped him out as he fell in and first responders had to rescue him! I laughed so hard that I forgot my pain and weakness. His stories were a welcome distraction and we were enjoying one another's company.

As lunch came to an end, Harrison said, "I'm leaving for a few days on a guys' weekend, but can I take you out again when I return?" We arranged to meet for dinner, and as I lay in bed that night, still feeling miserable, I smiled and thought of him.

Chapter 4

OUR FIRST DINNER DATE WAS at a small Italian restaurant on the Upper West Side. I learned that he was from a divorced family, he was the youngest of three kids, and he was born on the same day as his older brother. His mom did find love again, remarried, and had two more kids. His stepfather had four kids with his first wife, so his "blended family" counted nine kids altogether. They were all exceptionally well educated, each attending top-notch boarding schools in the northeast, and continuing on to prestigious Ivy League universities and New England small colleges. Harrison's father was also a presence in his life, and he too had another son, who was residing outside of the country. Additionally, Harrison had many cousins (whom he saw in the summers) and was extremely close to his paternal grandmother.

My head was spinning hearing all of this. I was properly impressed (and, maybe, jealous?) by his family's dedication to education. Previous to this, I'd never met anyone who went to a boarding school or to an Ivy League college, and, intellectually, I felt out of my league. But, sitting across from him, I noticed that he was completely open about the opportunities he had been given. Harrison's conversational approach was inviting and it certainly put me at ease. My impression of him was that he was solid in his presence and wise beyond his years.

Harrison learned that I was the oldest of four kids, that my parents divorced when I was five years old, and that my mom never remarried. My youngest brother and sister had different fathers from my brother and me. My father was around, and growing up we saw him every weekend, but now that we are older it's seldom. After I graduated from high school, I moved to New York, attended a performing-arts school, and was now pursuing a career in acting. My mother was one of ten children born to my maternal grandparents, and I also had many cousins. These ever-present grandparents had a huge influence in my life, in particular my grandmother. We ended the conversation by agreeing wholeheartedly with one another that our grandmothers were both beacons of light in our lives.

Harrison walked me home, and we had our first kiss! We were both conservative in our approach, I'm sure, for different reason. It was a gentle kiss, the only kiss up to that point in my life that I believe was met with mutual tenderness. He wished me good evening and asked if he could see me again.

No brainer. I said, "Yes!"

Imagine That!

As I put on my pajamas and curled up in front of the TV, I found myself thinking about Harrison and the differences between us. In this short time knowing him, my impression of him, unlike any guys I've met up to this point, is that he is very methodical and formal. I gathered that his upbringing had prepared him well for opportunities. When they were presented, they were met with his attitude to succeed in whatever he chose as a profession. First and foremost, I found him to be a self-assured gentleman.

He saw me as this tall (five foot seven), lean, brown-eyed black girl with lots of sassiness. I wore my hair short, inspired by the model Linda Evangelista. Most of the compliments I got were on my smile. Fortunately for me, I was blessed with straight teeth. Otherwise, we could not have afforded braces. Because of my upbringing, I lived life through limited experiences brought on by a spontaneous, nothing-to-lose attitude. Barely above the poverty line and one paycheck away from living with my grandparents, what did I have to lose? Whatever I chose for a profession could only be an improvement, especially if I worked hard. Unfortunately, I didn't have role models that represented educators, doctors, lawyers, entrepreneurs, and corporate America. "Get a job" was the message! But what job? Any job? The men in my family mostly worked in construction, and the women in either the food industry or retail.

As the week slowly progressed, when walking the streets of NY, while working, and during any down time, I started to wonder if the difference between us would soon make a difference. Racially, intellectually, and in terms of worldly experience.

Would he eventually become bored when the excitement was over?

Christine called mid-week, wanting to hang out, and I agreed to meet her after work. As I was gathering my things to leave, a coworker informed me that I had a phone call.

It was Harrison! "Hi, Brooke. I'm in the city! Would you like to meet up?"

My face almost cracked in half with a ridiculously huge smile as I replied, "I'd love to, Harrison!" and then, remembering my commitment to Christine, "I already have plans with Christine, but I'd love for you to join us both?" Harrison was game and agreed to meet us on the Upper East Side at a quaint bar.

Christine and I sat at the bar chatting away, and I was super excited to see Harrison. I was wearing my Norma Kamali navy-blue pinstriped pantsuit. My hair was slick backed, red lips, and pearl earrings. We sipped on rum-and-Cokes and munched on the popcorn that was placed there for the happy drinkers. Harrison soon walked in, wearing blue jeans and a baby-blue polo shirt that complemented his eyes. There was no mistaking when he entered the bar. His presence was grand and smooth, and he towered over everyone. My heart beat fast, because once he entered a room, he was noticed by all, but he walked straight over to us, leaned down, and gave me a kiss that said "I'm with her," then leaned over to Christine and gave her a hug.

"Hi, ladies, how are you? And what are you girls drinking?"

Harrison didn't have to get the bartender's attention because he too had noticed Harrison immediately when he walked in. He waited for the greetings to be over and asked Harrison what he would like for a drink.

Harrison ordered a beer on tap. The three of us enjoyed the music and vibes at the bar and talked mostly about the waning summer. I couldn't get over how two and a half hours passed so quickly and was sorry the night had to end. Christine had to travel back to Hoboken, and Harrison was meeting up with Don, his best friend. Harrison walked us both to the curb and hailed a cab. Once the cab arrived, Christine got in, and she and Harrison said their goodbyes. Harrison stood a foot taller than me, so I looked up to him as he placed his right hand on my cheek ever so gently and leaned in to give me a long kiss goodnight. It was passionate but tasteful in front of Christine.

As Christine and I continued on to my apartment before she headed back to NJ, she spoke very highly of Harrison.

"He seems like such a good guy, Brooke."

"Believe me, I think he's amazing too," I conceded. "I must admit that I am a little insecure about dating him, though. We were practically raised on separate planets – financially and educationally, not to mention our obvious racial difference."

"Uhhh…I'm pretty sure that Harrison noticed you were black before he asked you out," returned Christine. "And he doesn't seem to have a problem with any of this, so why do you?"

Harrison and I met later in the week for dinner and, as I was still feeling a bit insecure, I was nervous. Harrison was his usual charming self, and our evening was so comfortable that I didn't realize until later how easy it was to have an adult conversation of substance with him. We really seemed to have a unique way of communicating. No pretense, no judgments, just effortless and meaningful conversation. I was always amazed that I genuinely made him laugh.

As the night ended, Harrison asked if I was available to go out the following week. Obviously, I said yes, completely unconcerned about the casual manner in which we were scheduling our dates. I was occasionally

Imagine That!

still dating other people and I assumed he was as well. At the same time, I really enjoyed talking to him and I didn't want it to end. His ability to communicate was new to me. (I loved it!) And I assumed he was enjoying my company too. Harrison and I went out on a few more dates like this, and we were feeling the chemistry that was happening between us. I'd learned that he was going through a transition in starting a new job and wrapping up his own company.

He started picking me up from work quite regularly, and this did not escape the notice of my coworkers. My attempt at a calm, cool approach was decimated when my boss volunteered, "Brooke, we can all see how much you like him!" I started paying attention to my appearance before leaving work just in case he called and said he was in town…which was happening a lot more.

One night, we were chatting, and Harrison said, "Would you like to join me for a quiet weekend away? My grandmother has a home in the countryside of New Jersey. She is away for the summer, but encourages me to use it when I am able."

Could he see my excitement? I was about to jump out of my seat into his lap.

"I'd like that," I answered with a smile.

He smiled back.

Always a perfect gentleman, Harrison arrived at my apartment precisely on time. I was waiting for him in the lobby of my building, wearing blue jeans, a silk Versace shirt that was part of one of my uniforms, and green suede mules. He loaded my bag into a car he fondly called the "banana boat," an old blue station wagon from the *Brady Bunch* era that had previously belonged to his grandmother. This was one of Harrison's most attractive qualities; he was always unassuming. It would be an understatement to say I was looking forward to the next two days. Harrison and me, alone in the countryside? Oh boy! I was more than ready for our relationship to take the next step, and by the way he was looking at me, I was positive he was too.

We drove about an hour out of NY across a truly beautiful rural landscape. Stopping at the general store in this small town, we bought a few items to make ourselves dinner and breakfast. Eventually we arrived at the property, and at the end of a long dirt road sat a gorgeous house. Harrison parked in front of this beautiful house, precede to get our bags out of the car and unlocked the door. Upon entering the house, I was speechless. It was absolutely magical. The foyer alone was as big as my studio apartment. There was a fireplace in the entry hall large enough for a small child to stand in. To the left was a red-carpeted grand staircase that wound around to the second floor. The formal dining room was enormous, easily the size of four small bedrooms. It contained a black piano, a round table that comfortably accommodated ten Hitchcock chairs, and an antique swinging door that connected this room to the kitchen. But all of this finery was overshadowed by the mural painted around the entire room: an African river landscape with native Africans having lunch. I realized my mouth was hanging open, and as I quickly regained my composure, I turned back to Harrison's running commentary: "…and the mural was painted by my grandmother." The tour continued through a living room, a sitting room, two offices, and a bathroom. The floors were a dark, wide-plank wood, and beautiful multi-colored drapes warmly cloaked the windows in every antique-filled room. Wow, I was blown away.

As I searched for the appropriate words to adequately convey my compliments for the home, Harrison remained quite humble. He simply said, "Well, this is my grandmother's place, and someday I hope to have something like this." You could tell he adored her and was very grateful that she allowed him to stay there while she was on holiday.

That night, we cooked dinner together, each trying to navigate our way in the kitchen. We dined on the back porch by candlelight and talked until we couldn't talk anymore.

He shared with me that his company that he shared with another partner was going under because he'd learned by accident, with his brother, that the partner was embezzling funds and using them for personal use and not paying the bills. His company was a popcorn business that used the actual corn-on-the-cob, which you placed in the microwave to be popped. Great idea, but the business failed due to his partner's improper use of funds.

I learned that as Harrison's grandparents traveled the world, one of the many places they visited was Africa. Through his grandfather's job came many opportunities for them to meet important people. One of them was the emperor of Ethiopia, Haile Selassie, who ruled that country from 1930 to 1974. Apparently, his grandmother, whom Harrison called Gran, fell in love with Africa, admiring their traditions and style. She was so inspired that she painted her dining-room mural of a mystical celebration of two kings having lunch together to celebrate their freedom and not having communists take over where the Blue and White Nile meet in Africa.

There was a comfort with Harrison that I'd never experienced before, and as we slowly made our way upstairs, the comfort that I had experienced during dinner was fading. My obvious attraction for Harrison began to feel an awful lot like nervousness. What were his expectations? Would I disappoint him and ruin the relationship we'd built so far?

My bag had been placed in a gorgeous, canary-yellow bedroom with a private bathroom attached. It was exactly how I imagined an expensive hotel would look. The remainder of the upstairs consisted of more guest rooms, and a breathtaking master suite. Hands downs, the most amazing thing (besides the dining-room mural) was Harrison's grandmother's closet. She had a dressing room in her closet and a SHOE WALL! I loved this woman already. Like the rest of the house, her bedroom was full of warmth, love, style, and history. I could not wait to see everything again in the daylight.

"Make yourself at home, Brooke," said Harrison as he returned to the yellow room. "Take a bath and unwind if you like? I'll clean up downstairs."

"I think I'll take you up on that," I answered. I needed some time to calm my nerves and consider what was absolutely going to happen – HARRISON AND I WERE GOING TO HAVE SEX!

As I wallowed in the warm waters and bubbles of Crabtree & Evelyn in my bathtub, I gave myself a reality check. "Okay, self. Here's how this could go down: 1) Harrison and I will have sex and it will be great and we will have more dates. 2) Harrison and I will have sex and it will be disappointing and I will never hear from him again."

Per usual, I was worrying about "what might be," instead of just allowing the natural progression to happen.

Harrison returned to my room, and we gently started kissing, touching each other passionately, and he simply asked, "Brooke, can I make love to you?"

I drank in his six-foot-four frame and his honest face. "Yes," I whispered nervously.

His gentle kisses turned to mutual passion as my body responded to his touch, moving in perfect rhythm and exploding with affection. The night was magical. Exquisite, I might add. Harrison was respectful and attentive in every sense of the word.

Lord, help me. I was falling in love.

The next morning I made a concentrated effort to not be self-conscious. In the past, I'd struggled with my expectations after intimacy, and I still had twenty-four hours here with Harrison. After breakfast, we took a long walk on the hundred-plus-acre property. Some of the land was still used for farming and Harrison showed me the pond where, as a boy, he'd learned to ice skate. We passed the remainder of the day lounging, reading, and making love again, and by evening, we were settled back on the porch for a second candlelight dinner.

I was most surprised by how he checked in with me on how I was feeling now that we had made love. He said, "I enjoyed every bit of last night, and I hope you did as well?" He continued by saying I was very sexy and that dance had served me well.

I assumed he meant he liked my moves or that I was fit physically and laughed. I told him, "Yes, I enjoyed every bit of last night, and you playing three sports like hockey, lacrosse, and football makes a girl feel pretty protected."

It was comforting to know he cared. The next morning, he drove me back to the city. I could not remember the last time I had been so relaxed.

Chapter 5

(Fall 1991)

After being in the country for two days, I returned home to a full answering machine. Returning calls was a great distraction, but I couldn't control my excitement, so I called Christine first. I shared with her everything. She seemed very supportive, although she was not having much luck with guys lately. My nervous anticipation came later that night when Harrison called. His focus was all about ME.

"How are YOU? And did you enjoy the country? And can I see you later this week?"

Did he seriously think I would say no?

"I was hoping maybe we could go ice skating?" he said.

I'd never been ice skating before, but growing up I would roller skate on Sunday nights. "Why not?" I conceded.

"Would you mind if I included my sister in the invitation?" asked Harrison.

I was actually thrilled at this suggestion. Harrison's sister, Celine, lived in the city and was also pursuing a career in acting.

The three of us met at an ice rink on the West Side of Manhattan. Harrison introduced us, and immediately her similarities to Harrison were apparent: she was polite, tall (about six feet), blonde, and had the same captivating smile and confident presence.

Harrison skated onto the ice first, and I must say, it was one of the sexiest sights I'd ever seen! Oh my God, he was a vision! I knew he played hockey in college, but I had no idea that there would be something so attractive about seeing a big, handsome guy skate so gracefully. I, on the other hand, looked very awkward. Much like her brother, Celine was graceful on the ice, and her ability as a skater was more than admirable. She was a natural teacher, and actually had the patience to show me how to balance on the blade. Without Celine, neither my ass nor my ego would have endured the evening!

I enjoyed being with Celine and connected with her in a way that made me easily imagine us becoming friends. We commiserated, in particular, about the frustrating process of getting jobs in acting. At the end of the evening, we wished one another luck with auditions, and I really, not so secretly, hoped to see her again.

Imagine That!

One random afternoon, Harrison and I sat in front of an ice-cream parlor, enjoying cones and people watching. My sweet tooth was in rapture, and one hundred percent of my attention was on my scoop of chocolate-chip cookie dough, so I did not notice the serious expression on Harrison's face.

"Brooke, I have a question to ask you."

"Sure," I said casually while stuffing the last bite of cone into my mouth.

"Will you be my girlfriend?"

Was the sugar going straight to my head or did he just seriously and officially ask me to be his girlfriend? I swallowed uncomfortably and turned to look at him. He was definitely serious. My first instinct was to jump into his lap and cover his handsome face with kisses, but that little voice, that familiar, nagging voice in my head, would not allow me this unexpected joy.

I looked into Harrison's eyes and lamely replied, "Can I think about that for a few days?" WHAT THE FUCK WAS I SAYING? Being Harrison's one and only official girlfriend was beyond my wildest dreams!

Harrison softened. "Sure. But can I ask why?" He was not angry. He was not offended. He had no agenda or pre-determined rebuttal. He simply wanted know what my concerns were. This amazing, lovely man wanted to know me. The real me. The flawed me. The fearful, insecure me.

"Here goes nothing," I said to myself. I took a deep breath and began to share.

"Harrison, I am afraid of losing you. You are the best man I've ever met and I can see myself falling hard for you. My fear is that, as time goes on, our differences will become more evident and more mountainous. I'm not sure how I could recover from your rejection if things did not work out."

Harrison smiled. "Brooke, I hear you. I fear taking a chance with my feelings as well, but to not attempt going forward with you is even scarier. Our differences will never be larger than our emotional connection can overcome." He continued stating that he had dated outside his race before me while attending college and after. And for whatever reason, it did not work out, and certainly not because they were racially different.

I looked at him with disbelief.

"Take all the time you need," he said.

Alone, later that afternoon, I dug deep. Racially, intellectually, and economically, Harrison and I were polar opposites. What did I really have to offer him? My insecurities over my lack of education? My limited exposure to the world and to intelligent company? My small-town-limited influence? What I knew for sure was my core being was God, family, and enduring love. I knew that I was confident, ambitious, kind, and attractive, but could my strengths of character and physical attributes be enough to carry us through darkness when the brightness of love dimmed?

I needed a sounding board. I called Christine and excitedly told her about Harrison's question and followed up with my personal list of "buyer beware" negative qualities.

"Seriously, Brooke, interracial worries? I have seen the way Harrison looks at you."

(What? Up to this point, I'd had no idea he had a "look" that was just for me!)

"Who the hell would even question a guy of Harrison's size and stature over his ethnic choice in women? Girl! Are you forgetting we live in NYC and not some Podunk backwoods racist shithole? Open your eyes!"

God, I loved Christine – mouth of a sailor and heart of a saint.

Truth be told, I had once been the victim of a painful small-minded mentality during my high-school years. A white guy from my class and I had mutual feelings for one another and were exploring the possibility of dating, until one afternoon, I received a dreadful phone call. He said he had spoken to his parents and his pastor from church and told them about our mutual feelings for one another. After much discussion, the consensus among the adults was that he and I were "too different," and "would never make it" as a couple. P.S. End of conversation and end of the relationship. I bounced back slowly from that rejection by dating a nice gentleman, who later went into the NFL and was quite successful.

Christine was very supportive, and I valued her opinion. She, too, was from a small town and recognized that with small towns often come small-town values.

"It comes down to this," said Christine. "You and Harrison have a way of communicating unlike anything I have ever witnessed. Brooke, he makes you laugh, and you are ACTUALLY glowing! Why wouldn't you take a chance on love?"

Why wouldn't I? This city had already changed me in so many ways and had opened my eyes to possibilities I never could have imagined. The energy of NYC was itself a constant feedback of inspiration. I actively sought out culture, went to museums, and "accidentally" became an avid reader. As a to-and-from work commuter, I joined my contemporaries in devouring the *NY Times*, the latest best-selling novels, and magazines on every topic, from fashion to news. My reading career was initially ignited by Alice Walker's book, *Possessing the Secret of Joy*. I enjoyed being engaged in the fabric of readers, and socially, it made me feel connected.

Funnily enough, I did not have much time to reflect on or think about his question, nor to reflect upon my answer, because later that night, Harrison called.

"I changed my mind. I can't wait. What's your answer?"

Imagine That!

To my great relief, we simultaneously burst out laughing. Truthfully, I didn't want to wait any longer, either.

"Yes, I would love nothing more than to be your girlfriend!"

As we said goodnight, I could imagine Harrison smiling at me through the phone.

I was on cloud nine! I sat there in my apartment feeling great and scared all at once. And then the panic set in. My failsafe remedy for panic: call Mom!!!

As I furiously dialed her number, I didn't even realize how late it was. She answered my call with alarm in her voice. "Brooke? What's wrong?"

"Nothing's wrong, Mom. But I need to talk," I said.

"It's almost midnight, Brooke."

"But, Mom, I met a guy. We have been dating for about three months and I think things are starting to get serious," I blurted out. "I need to tell you all about him."

"Now? Right now?" she asked.

"Yes, Mom, right now."

She could hear the nervousness in my voice, and she calmly asked, "Do you really like this guy, Brooke?"

"Yes, I do. I really like him," I replied.

"Well then, trust that your family will like him as well. Go to bed, and you can tell me all about your guy in the morning. Goodnight, honey." And she was gone.

I was speechless. Based solely on my opinion, had my mom just given her blessing to a guy she'd never met?

Early the next day, I called my mom. She listened patiently while I shared with her every detail I could – from how Harrison and I met to everything I knew about him and his family. Eventually the discussion came around to my insecurities and concerns over our differences. Her thoughts basically echoed Christine's – the world was changing for the better, and Harrison and I were a part of that change. She left me with two simple pieces of advice:

"Brooke, stay true to yourself, never stop communicating with one another, and the rest will figure itself out."

The conversation with my mom was reassuring and comforting. Officially together! I was feeling sooo good.

A few days later, I met Harrison after work. We were sitting and chatting when suddenly it dawned on me that I had made plans (months previously) to see a Knicks basketball game with my friend, Jay. The date was fast approaching and I mentioned to Harrison that I would be attending the game on Tuesday night.

"Who is taking you to the game?" asked Harrison.

"My friend Jay," I answered.

Harrison grew quiet, and then very matter-of-factly said, "Brooke, I think you may have my intentions for this relationship all wrong. I don't want my girlfriend going on dates with other guys."

"I asked him to take me months ago," I replied. "I feel obligated to go with him."

Harrison was calm and chose his words carefully. "I will take you to the game if it's important to you, but no girlfriend of mine is going out with another guy. If you are serious about us, I would like you to call Jay, cancel the date, and tell him that you are in a relationship."

"Okay," I responded.

This conversation was a real wake-up call for me. Harrison was confirming our relationship to be one of mutual respect, straightforward communication, and trust. He was not threatening me, nor playing games, but simply requesting that I treat him like my boyfriend. No problems here!

I called Jay the following morning and told him that I would not be attending the game with him, and why. He was understanding and wished me well in my relationship.

And for the record, Harrison did not take me to the Knicks game, but substituted tickets to the NY Rangers hockey game instead. I LOVED IT!

Chapter 6

HARRISON AND I WERE FINDING our way together. We began by seeing each other a lot more during the week, as he was busy looking for a job, wrapping up loose ends at his company, and searching for a new job, while I'd been auditioning and was landing jobs as an extra. One successful audition landed me on the set of *Malcolm X*, starring Denzel Washington and directed by Spike Lee. This small role as an extra (commuting near the subway) was so exciting! Similarly, I was employed in a scene that Spike Lee also filmed in Bloomingdale's for *Jungle Fever*. (I kept that pay stub as a souvenir.)

My new routine was to let Harrison know where I was filming for the day, and he would meet me at the location and escort me home. I loved having him around and available to me, and our hours spent together often went well into the mornings.

As a new couple we were having a blast introducing one another to our friends. We eventually had a standing "couples date" every Wednesday night with one of Harrison's friends, Randy, and his wife, Hillary. She

Imagine That!

worked for the *New Yorker* magazine, and every week our foursome tried a new restaurant or bar that Hillary was writing about for the magazine.

Harrison's best friend, Donnie A, who was also his roommate in New Jersey, became one of our most constant companions. It was evident that the friendship between them was always entertaining, as both were smart, funny, quick-witted, and knew how to have a good time. Coincidentally, Donnie A was the same friend that had given Harrison the "evil eye" the night we first met, and despite our ominous start, he gave me the nickname Sweet Pea… Christine would join us on a few occasions, and she too found them to be quite the pair.

The roommates finally decided that it was time to move into NYC proper, and since Harrison was still looking for work, the burden of finding a place fell to him. When my scheduled permitted, I often helped him look and offered my opinions. One day in particular, his appointments started at 7:30 a.m. Downtown in the Financial District of Manhattan. I thought the apartment was too dark, and so we continued the search from Downtown to the Lower East Side to Midtown, viewing apartments that were large, small, walk-up, old, new…nonstop until about four p.m. I finally said to Harrison, "I need a break and some food." He agreed and we stumbled into a cozy eatery called Rath Bones that had wood chips all over the floor. We sat at the

45

bar and ordered some well-earned burgers and Cokes. I was so involved in eating my burger that at first I didn't notice that Harrison was staring at me.

"Thank you for today," he said gently.

I could sense that he desperately wanted to say something more, but we both just continued eating our meals. My guard was up; I immediately went to the dark side. In my nervous haste, I was thinking to myself, RED FLAG! He is moving into the city, he's in the market for a new job, and the last thing he needs is a girlfriend. Harrison was scheduled to see two more apartments, but I decided to go home, as I was meeting Christine and Eleanor that night. He had plans to see Don and friends later, so we said our goodbyes and looked forward to seeing each other the following night.

After I left him, went home, showered, and got in my PJs, I called Christine and Eleanor to cancel our night out. I was exhausted, and I barely moved from my bed for the next three hours until I heard the phone ring. I decided to let the answering machine get it, and then I heard Harrison's voice.

"Hi, Brooke. It's me. I just wanted to say thank you again for taking the time to be with me today. It was great having you with me in the daunting task of looking for an apartment. I hope you have a fun night out and I miss – "

I picked up the phone receiver. "Hi."

Imagine That!

He was surprised to hear my voice. "I thought you were out with the girls and I wanted to leave you a sweet message to come home to."

"I cancelled with the girls and was just relaxing. I didn't know how exhausting looking for apartments could be!"

"Would you like to join Donnie A and me?"

They were in my area, so I hoisted myself off the couch and joined them at a bar a block away. I walked in and, of course, they had command of the bar with girls all around them. The troop gave me a huge greeting, making me feel special while simultaneously disappointing the pack of groupies they had accumulated.

Harrison and I eventually decided to leave the gathering, and left Donnie to hold court with the ladies, any one of them ready to drop their panties at Donnie's request.

We were traveling along a crowded Amsterdam Ave. when Harrison suddenly stopped walking, turned to face me, and looked directly into my eyes. I had the same nervous feeling from earlier in the day, and as I looked back at him, he said it. "I love you."

I was completely shocked and surprised to hear my own voice saying, "I love you, too."

Harrison wrapped his arms around me, lifted me up, and started swinging me around in the middle of the street! All joyful and lost in bliss, we captured the attention of pedestrians who were just trying to get around us, which our PDA was making impossible. I didn't care. I was in love and it felt great!

Being in love with Harrison and knowing that he loved me back felt like nothing I had ever experienced – safe, effortless, and mutual. I never doubted that this moment, when Harrison confessed his love for me, and I for him, I would cherish forever.

Shortly thereafter, Harrison invited me to join him for a repeat weekend back to the country at his grandmother's house.

"My father and his girlfriend will be there. Would you like to meet them?" asked Harrison.

"I guess you could twist my arm!" I immediately conceded. I adored his grandmother's home, and Harrison had made me feel so comfortable, loved, and supported that the idea of meeting his family felt natural.

Mike and Polly greeted us at the door with welcoming smiles and bear hugs. His father was as tall as Harrison, with a deep voice and a presence bigger than life – I felt like I was meeting an old friend. It was evident that Mike loved his son deeply and unconditionally, and that it probably would not have mattered whom Harrison had brought to meet him.

We prepared for a tasty barbecue dinner on the porch, as Polly loved to cook, and really knew her way

Imagine That!

around the kitchen. I helped out with the smaller jobs, and eventually we all settled in to eat by candlelight. A natural storyteller, Mike kept us entertained with anecdotes and tales into the evening. Polly shared with me her love of books, and I enjoyed how easy it was to talk to her. I never felt like an outsider, or a new girlfriend; it was as if I'd known them for quite some time.

Donnie A showed up the next night, and our quiet country weekend became a party. The house was filled with outrageous laughter, drinks, and schoolboy banter. I felt perfectly at home.

That weekend left me thinking about my dad and how close he and I were. My dad is a soft-spoken, mild-mannered guy, who, in my opinion, was currently experiencing some rough times.

Growing up, my brother and I would look forward to spending weekends with my dad. Saturday mornings, he would take us fishing and crabbing, and in the fall, we would usually watch college football games on Saturday. One of my oldest memories is of watching a game with my dad where Boston College quarterback Doug Flutie threw a Hail Mary and connected with his receiver at the end of the fourth quarter to win the game. It was exciting to witness, and my dad jumped up off the couch and shouted, "What a finish! Did you see that?" Since then, I would forever love football.

Another experience with my dad that actually had a huge impact on me was the year of my eighth-grade school dance. My friend Samantha and I wanted to attend the dance and my father agreed to take us and pick us up. I remember the whole ride there telling them both how I was going to enter the dance contest and WIN the sixty dollars of the prize money. I wanted the money so badly, because I wanted to buy myself some Gloria Vanderbilt jeans with the red stitching. He was flabbergasted with my confidence and spent the entire thirty-minute car ride gently trying to convince me not to get my hopes up. My dad actually said, "You are not going to win."

"And why not?" I asked. Someone had to win.

"You are a minority at this school, Brooke." He went on to explain to me the difference between racial minority and the majority. All this dialogue of difference was not interesting to me, at all. I actually thought it was the dumbest reason for not succeeding that I'd ever heard. I was banking on my talent, and I was not at all threatened by my competition, especially for the reason he gave. Well, when the dance was over at eleven p.m., I was in the parking lot, running to my father and yelling, "I won! I won! I won!" I could tell he felt badly, yet proud at the same time.

"I'll never tell you that you can't succeed again, Brooke," he promised.

Imagine That!

One Friday night, my dad and stepmom took us out to dinner. I remember I ordered a steak and was using the utensils incorrectly. My dad immediately stopped me and said, "Let me teach you how to use a knife and fork properly." He continued, "Most people don't know how to use a knife and fork, and it looks awkward. Learning the proper way will serve you well in life." I never wanted the weekends to end, as they felt like a postcard family. I also enjoyed being with my stepmom; she never had children of her own, but she always treated my brother and me with love.

All of this led me to my dad's current behavior, which was bewildering to me. He had been going through some sort of unattractive changes, and then informed me that he and my stepmom, after twelve years marriage, were divorcing. I was so sad, and with no details forthcoming, I eventually had the courage to ask him, "Why are you choosing to end this marriage?"

His response to me was, "Everyone must lead their own lives and make their own choices. We must take chances as long as we don't hurt ourselves or others." What the hell did that mean? He was hurting me! Selfishly, I didn't want him to divorce my stepmom.

Chapter 7

(November 1991)

As the weeks went on, Harrison and I hit our stride and settled into a fairly consistent routine. I loved being his girlfriend and calling him "MY boyfriend" gave me an embarrassing amount of self-satisfaction.

I loved the people that I worked with, especially one guy in particular, Glenn. He and I worked side by side every Sunday (he for Calvin Klein and I for Versace) at Bloomingdale's. Glenn was like a big brother to me, and I felt comfortable talking to him about everything. He always gave me realistic advice on auditions, jobs, and, my favorite subject, Harrison! It wasn't until after a year of working together that I realized Glenn was gay. I honestly had not even considered his sexuality, nor did it make any difference in our friendship. Knowing him taught me that people are unique and different, and whatever I had imagine "gay" was was completely askew. Through loving Glenn, I learned that respecting one another, in similarities and differences, allowed the commonality in humanity to prevail. Glenn was a true friend to me.

One Sunday evening after work, I received a call from Harrison.

"Hi, babe. How was your day?"

"Great," I said, "except that I'm missing you."

"I echo your thoughts entirely," agreed Harrison.

Usually when we wanted to see other, Harrison would drive into the city to get me, but on this particular Sunday, he had been watching football with Donnie, and had already had a couple of drinks. He asked if I'd take the bus out to see him instead, and since I was not working on Monday, I agreed. I took the subway to Port Authority, hopped on the bus to NJ, and in just over an hour, I was knocking on his front door. For about fifteen minutes, I knocked, and knocked, and knocked, but Harrison did not answer the door. I started to panic – I could hear the TV, but wasn't sure if he was in there. Was he asleep? What should I do? I continued knocking for another fifteen minutes before going across the street to call him from the pay phone. I was livid! There was not a soul out on the street, and as the phone continued to ring, unanswered, many horrific thoughts raced through my mind. Do I hang up? Now my panic was in overdrive… Do I wait another forty minutes on the street for the return bus back to Manhattan? Do I go back and bang on the door some more? I angrily dialed the phone once again, and after about eight rings, Harrison answered!

"Ahh…ohhh…uh…hello?" he said sleepily.

"ARE YOU KIDDING ME, HARRISON?!" I was pissed! "I am across the street, at the gas station, by myself, in the dark, and have been for over forty-five minutes!"

"Brooke! Oh my God! I am so sorry!" In a flash he was outside and apologizing profusely. "I fell asleep…I lost track of time…please, Brooke."

I glared back at him, his hair disheveled and his eyes wide. Why did he even invite me if he was so exhausted? I was tired too, but had managed the journey out to see him. I wanted to engage him in an argument, but I did not. I just passed him, dropped my stuff in his room, monopolized his bathroom, crawled into his bed, and went to sleep. My silence was the most effective punishment I could muster.

The next morning, I woke up to Harrison's worried face staring at me from the side of the bed. He was dressed and had been out already. Again, he began by apologizing for his lack of consideration. He then took my hand and placed something in my palm.

"While you were sleeping I went out and duplicated my apartment key. I never ever want this to happen again."

Imagine That!

I just looked at him, shaking my head. "You're right. It's not going to happen again." I said, reliving the nightmare in my head.

The key was shiny and warm from his grip, and it meant more to me than his hundred apologies ever could. I slowly softened toward him, and we ended up enjoying the day, by passionately making love and eventually having a laugh about the incident. We took a long walk to the park, had a late lunch, and Harrison drove me back to NY. In my entire life up to this point, I had never felt so close to a man. Not only was I in love with Harrison, but we were becoming best friends.

The holidays, fast approaching, were always the busiest season of the retail year. "Time off" in this business was unheard of in November and December, and I would not be traveling home to see my family. Harrison and Celine were going upstate to visit their mom, Philly, as she was hosting Thanksgiving dinner for her four sisters and their families. His plan was to leave on Wednesday and return Sunday night. I would be working, but Christine, Eleanor, and I, along with a few of their co-workers planned a dinner together. As mid-November flew by, Harrison asked me if I would consider joining him and his family for Thanksgiving? He had obviously been doing his research, and suggested that, if I left with him on Wednesday evening, we could enjoy Thanksgiving

Day together, and then I could take the Amtrak train back to the city early Friday morning in time for opening. It would be a lot of traveling for the one and a half nights, but we both agreed the effort was worth us being together. When I ran the idea by Christine and Eleanor, they encouraged me to go, and decided to rest instead of cook.

The added benefit to accepting Harrison's invitation was that I would finally meet his mom and some of his extended family. As I said earlier, I was no stranger to large families, and I did not feel intimidated by the thought of invading a large group of cousins, aunts, and uncles. On any given day throughout my childhood, my grandmother's house would be filled with a similar cast of relatives. Harrison confirmed the invite with his mom and stepdad, and the next thing I knew, he, Celine, and I were on a three-and-a-half-hour road trip up to Saratoga Springs. At one point during the trip, Celine fell asleep, and Harrison noticed that I was particularly quiet.

"You okay?" asked Harrison.

"I don't know, actually. I am feeling nervous and slightly concerned," I replied.

"You aren't back on the interracial couple thing, are you?" said Harrison.

"No, funnily enough. I rarely even think about that anymore. I am intimidated about how I will hold a conversation with all the intellectuals in your family," I admitted.

Secretly, I was feeling insecure about my level of education, and for this group, a high-school diploma and performing-arts degree would not be enough. I continued to mentally list the impressive educational stats of Harrison's family: His mother graduated magna cum laude from Radcliffe college (Harvard) at the top of her class. Women were not allowed to be called Harvard graduates until 1964! All five of her kids attended the most exclusive boarding schools in the US and continued on to graduate from the highest-rated universities and colleges. Harrison's cousins, similarly, had gone to Andover boarding school and graduated from Yale. Even the youngest cousins were in private middle school.

"What am I going to discuss with everyone?" I worried.

"Babe, the environment will be very relaxed. I am exceptionally close with my family – you'll be just fine," said Harrison.

I smiled and tried to take encouragement from his words. At about 11:30 p.m., we arrived at an impressive white Victorian house with a wraparound porch. Celine woke up, thanked Harrison for driving, and got out of the car. Harrison grabbed my hand, as he could see I was panicked.

He said, "Nothing matters but you and me, and we are in this together." He looked into my eyes and squeezed my hand even harder. "We are solid."

I squeezed back and repeated to him, "Solid."

I tried to relax myself, but the butterflies consumed my stomach. We walked in the front door, and Harrison's cousin Chris was waiting for us. After hugs and introductions, we proceeded into the kitchen. There were plates of leftover dinner awaiting us, and a note from Philly explaining that she was too tired to wait up, but that she looked forward to seeing us in the morning. (Baked grits, a salad, and a roasted chicken! Oh my, I knew then that I could at least talk to her about food!) Like Harrison had promised, Chris was easy to talk to. He was relaxed and cool, and I didn't once think about my education.

The next morning was a full onslaught of introductions and a delicious breakfast in the cozy kitchen. As aunts, uncles, and cousins filled their plates with eggs, bacon, and sourdough toast, they caught up on one another's lives. Harrison's younger brother, Nick, was home from St. Paul's boarding school, and his younger sister, Abigail, was home from Milton Academy boarding school. Everyone was gentle in the questions they asked about my relationship with Harrison, and the family chatter among them created a nice buffer for me to ease in whatever I felt most comfortable. Then in came Harrison's mom, and my heart began racing a mile a minute. She hugged Harrison, welcomed me warmly, and asked, "How was the drive? Did you get a chance to eat some dinner last night?' She was great! And before we could really get into a deep conversation, someone would interrupt or greet us, or ask her questions about the plans of the day or about setting the table. The entire day was filled with the task of meeting his family, and later a nice walk into town to build an appetite for Thanksgiving dinner.

When we would gather at my grandmother's house for a large dinner, we would serve ourselves buffet style, and the children's plates were assembled first. Adults walked around, chatted continuously, and landed wherever there was space. Thanksgiving dinner at Harrison's mom's house was the complete opposite – a formal, intimate affair, with assigned seating.

I had the pleasure of sitting next to one of Harrison's aunts on one side, and his stepfather, Sam, on the other. They were both amazing table mates, so gracious, inquisitive about me, and genuinely interested in my answers.

"Are you reading anything interesting?" asked his aunt.

"I just finished reading *Malcolm X*, by Alex Haley," I replied. This sparked an animated discussion, with Sam joining the conversation too. Someone I admired almost immediately, Sam was a natural-born storyteller and poet who was deeply passionate about humankind.

I could recognize his wisdom and sense that he knew much about diverse cultures and how the world operated. I discovered that Sam's life's work was with the civil rights, and that he had marched with the Rev. Dr. Martin Luther King, Jr. from Selma to Montgomery, Alabama, in March 1965. I was completely engrossed in his experience; he told me that it took them four days to complete the journey in the rain and mud, all while living in tents. After dessert, he showed me a picture of himself walking beside the Rev. Dr. Martin Luther King and his wife, Coretta Scott King. The photo was taken by Moneta Sleet, Jr., for *Ebony* magazine, and then reprinted in the 1988 *Life* magazine issue. He also shared that he was in Washington to attend the "I Have a Dream" speech. I was rightly impressed beyond words!

At some point during clean-up, Harrison and I reconnected. "I saw that you were enjoying the conversation at dinner," he offered quietly.

The smile on my face only reinforced his observations. I was in complete awe of his stepfather. After our jobs were finished, the entire family retired to the living room and voted to play charades. I tried really hard to get out of this, not because I didn't think it would be fun, but because I was surprisingly nervous to perform in front of his family. I'm usually a ham when the attention is on me. (I actually couldn't remember EVER playing charades before!) I eventually conceded, and when it was my

Imagine That!

turn, I had to act out the movie *My Own Private Idaho*. Could I have chosen a more difficult title? Suddenly, I was standing in front of all thirty-five of them, but they easily seemed like a hundred. I think it was Harrison's younger brother Nick who put that title in the hat. He saw that I was struggling up there, alone, in front of the group, and he eventually started guessing some of my motions. Finally, someone called it correctly and, whew, it was over!

After checking with Harrison's mom, I sequestered myself in another room to make a "Happy Thanksgiving" call to my family in Florida. Following the charades match, I needed some of my own family love (and perhaps a little reassurance?) to get me through the next fifteen hours.

My mom was encouraging. "Remember, Brooke. You come from a family of love, too. Don't you forget that." She described the events that were happening with my family members, and I pictured everyone at my grandmother's house. Thankfully, she reported, no one was acting crazy, and my mind turned to moments where the entertainment at home could be a cross between funny and not so funny, depending upon who was present and the amount of alcohol consumed. It was comforting to hear her voice.

Harrison's mom and I eventually found some time alone, and although slightly guarded, she was more than pleasant. She wanted to make sure I was enjoying myself and asked all sorts of motherly questions, like: Where I was from? Why was I in NY? How did Harrison and I meet? When I told her that I was from Florida, and was in the city, like Celine, pursuing an acting career, she mentioned that she was happy that I was able to join them for the holidays. She also sympathized with my acting search and stress involved in my chosen career. Before I could answer her third question, Harrison had joined us, and communicated to her that we met through friends. Although that was not the exact truth, I just went along with his story – the people he mentioned kept us talking on the bench the night we met.

Celine later found me amongst all the family commotion. I felt at ease in her company and reassured her that I was feeling welcome with her family. Celine's pleasure at my revelation was genuinely sincere; she was incapable of being anything other than true. At the end of the evening I was exhausted, and quite the same the next morning when I found myself being escorted, by Chris and Harrison, to the train station. I arrived before the opening of Black Friday at Bloomingdales, ready and excited for my nine-a.m.-to-nine-p.m. workday! This double shift had been my own choice, as it allowed me to take off the entire day on Saturday.

My coworkers (especially Glenn) grilled me on meeting Harrison's family, and I gave them general details on the large group. Vocalizing my feelings for and experiences with them brought about some unexpected realizations. The genuine nature of Harrison, not to mention his tenderness toward the people he loved, was amazing and more evident than ever. The weekend flew by with long hours and many phone calls from Harrison, and we planned to see each other again on Monday. He seemed especially pleased to inform me that his family had really enjoyed meeting me.

I thought to myself, "Hmm, really? I'll take that!"

I was just happy to be informed that I'd made a good impression.

Chapter 8

DECORATIONS, LIGHTS, AND MUSIC HERALDED the arrival of December in NYC. The energy of the holidays drove my long shifts at Bloomingdale's. Not only had Harrison and Donnie found an apartment in Manhattan's Lower East Side, Harrison would also start his new job at Chase in the High Yield department. Both to begin in the New Year.

One evening we were having dinner when Harrison said, "I've been talking to my grandmother about you, and she would like us to come out to visit her one weekend." I, of course, had been hoping to meet her, as she was an important person in Harrison's life. He adored her and spoke of her frequently. My previous nervousness at meeting his mother reappeared three-fold just imagining meeting his grandmother. I did not want to disappoint either him or her.

I had recently become painfully aware of my lack of understanding of ethnicity in general. My boss at work, Nina, was practically an ethnicity specialist, and I tried to observe anything she pointed out while on the

Imagine That!

job. There were many times that I had no idea what the hell she was talking about – how could she tell someone was Jewish/Greek/Italian by the surname on their credit card? Little by little, I learned to recognize accents, speech, and commonalities in name spellings that would give me clues to someone's ethnic background. Funnily enough, through a discussion with Nina, I realized that my best friend from high school was Jewish! My childhood experience of ethnicity could be summarized into four categories: white, black, Asian, or Puerto Rican. Religion, nationality, and ancestry were, to me, unknown classifications.

Culturally aware, Nina was actually the one who'd brought Harrison's family's ethnicity to my attention.

"Oh my God!" squawked Nina. "You're meeting Harrison's WASP-y grandmother?! You should be terrified!"

Needless to say, her explanation of a White Anglo Saxon Protestant stereotype necessarily followed. And she was correct. I was terrified!

The big meet-up was scheduled for mid-December, and on that Friday, after work, Harrison and I headed out of the city.

The property and home were every bit as beautiful as I remembered, and as we pulled into the drive, she was at the door, waiting for us. She was very petite, with perfectly groomed white hair, wearing a blue skirt, a green blouse, and an Hermès scarf, and held a cane, just for balance. Harrison, towering over her, walked in first, and gently leaned down to give her a hug and a kiss. Her entire face beamed as he greeted her.

"Gran, this is Brooke," offered Harrison.

"Lovely to meet you. Thank you so much for inviting me, Mrs. Hitchcock." I followed Harrison's lead and also hugged her.

"Thank you for coming, and please call me Gran".

As Harrison brought in our bags, Gran directed him to take them to the beautiful canary-yellow room upstairs. The entire house smelled of home cooking.

"Make yourselves comfortable. I am heading upstairs for a bath and I will see you before dinner in the library at 7:30," said Gran. Then she proceeded up a private staircase (I had missed that at my last visit) into her part of the house.

Harrison and I walked upstairs and began rearranging our belongings. I also decided to take a bath before dinner – not only was it relaxing, but it divided the day from evening for me.

Afterward, I chose a dress that was conservative but flattering. A navy-blue V-neckline with cap sleeves. A pearl choker necklace and a three-strand pearl bracelet with multiple charms on it. Instead of a blazer or sweater, I wore my (work) Emanuel Ungaro red-rose scarf for warmth and color. As we headed to the library, we had to pass through the dining room. It was decorated exquisitely with lovely china, white table linens, beautiful fresh flowers, and candles. Once in the library, Gran introduced me to Ethan, her second husband. Shortly thereafter, Doris, the caretaker and cook, came in with vodka on the rocks with a twist of lemon for Gran and Ethan. Harrison and Doris made their pleasantries, and he introduced me before he slipped out and returned with glasses of red wine.

Gran and Ethan had married late in life, well after making eighty years in age. Both had lost their first spouses, and, luckily, found one another. It was beautiful to witness them holding hands, Ethan singing to her romantically as we settled into the library. Ethan wore dress slacks, a dress shirt, a tie, and a smoking jacket. For real! I had only seen men wear smoking jackets in old movies. Gran wore a beautiful dress, long to the floor, with pearls around her neck, matching earrings, and flat shoes. Her makeup was subtle, with rose lips. I thought she looked so elegant, and I later learned that she dressed like this for dinner nightly. Harrison, per usual, looked great, wearing cords with a dress shirt, tie, and sweater.

Gran and I began chatting, and I immediately felt so comfortable with her, as if she were my own grandmother.

She had a genuine warm tenderness about her, very approachable, with nothing but praises for me. Her questions were not probing in any way, just easy. I told her how much I loved her home. I complimented her on the amazing paintings, in particular the murals she had painted all over the house. She confided that she did not begin painting until she was well into her fifties, and that her sister, living nearby, was also an artist.

Apparently, most of the family was artistically inclined, as both of her daughters shared their mother's love of painting, and Harrison's dad was a sculptor.

Harrison and Ethan fell easily into talking about his new job-to-be in finance, his upcoming move to the city, and politics. Doris returned to the library to announce that dinner was ready, and when we walked into the dining room, all candles on the table and mantle were lit, and a toasty warmth radiated from the fireplace. Gran informed us that the menu consisted of filet mignon, artichokes, and potatoes, which all sounded great except I'd never had artichokes before. I whispered to Harrison that I'd never eaten artichokes while adding, "How do you even eat those pineapple-looking things?"

Reassuringly, he said, "Don't worry about it, just watch me."

Doris came back into the room and served Gran first, then me, and on to the men. After we all had our food on our plates, I watched them each pick an outer leaf from the artichoke, dip it into this amazing homemade hollandaise sauce, and scrape the meat from the inside of the leaf. To me, it was the same technique as eating a mango, and I was thinking to myself, "Okay...I got this."

Right as I was feeling secure, Harrison said, "Gran, Brooke has never eaten artichokes before." I was mortified! I shot him a death stare as I kicked him underneath the table.

Gran said, "Oh no, I'm so sorry to have them, as they are horrible and not in season. Please don't bother at even eating them because they're such a hassle." Her ability to make me feel comfortable was very motherly and I fell in love with her even more. (I did eat the artichokes!)

Once we were finished with dinner, Gran rang a tiny bell that was on the table near her. Doris came in and removed the dinner plates and returned with a chocolate cake that she placed in front of Gran. Gran sliced four pieces for us, and Doris came around with ice cream. Everything was civilized perfection, and I enjoyed every minute of conversation included.

After dinner, we said our goodnights. Harrison and I tried to watch some TV, but ended up upstairs, satisfied. In a failed attempt, I tried to express to Harrison how much I liked his grandmother, and how I understood (and seconded) his love for her. Words could not do my feelings justice. He said that he'd known she and I would relate to one another and were similar in many ways. All I knew when I went to bed was that nothing felt forced; Gran was authentically true and kind to me. I wanted to be around her and feel her calming presence. Gran was a warm, comforting blanket that had been placed over my body that I did not know I needed until it was in place. Imagine that?

We woke up the next morning to more delicious smells coming from the kitchen. A beautiful black woman, Geneva, greeted us with hot coffee and obvious joy at seeing Harrison. After introductions, she asked us what we would like for breakfast. Geneva had worked for Harrison's family for over thirty years, and her infectious, jolly laugh complemented the eggs and bacon perfectly. We sat in the dining room and Harrison and I continued our "Gran Mutual Admiration Society" conversation from the night before. After breakfast, Harrison and I got dressed and took a long walk around the property.

Upon our return, Gran was finishing her breakfast while she read the *NY Times*. We joined her at the table, and the three of us sat looking south at the pond. It was so relaxing there, just chatting and enjoying the view, that we lost track of time… Before we knew it, Geneva had prepared lunch for us in the dining room. She brought out some crackers and cheese that had been toasted in the oven with bowls of consommé soup. (A quick study, I did NOT mention to Harrison that I had never had consommé before!) We easily passed the remainder of the day reading, napping, and an afternoon delight of love making!

Imagine That!

That evening, Gran had invited her daughter Mai and her husband, Pete, who also lived on the property, to join us. They were an unforgettable couple, as it was the first time in my life that I'd spoken about anything "alternative." They were well-read and introduced me to many quirky ideas about living "outside the box." For the second time that day we lost track of time and did not realize the lateness of the hour until Ethan announced that he was turning in for the night. As I curled up in the bed of the beautiful canary room, I had the feeling of acceptance and welcome.

On Sunday morning, I joined Gran and Ethan at their local church service. After church, Gran invited her sister, Elizabeth, and her husband to lunch, bringing us to a party of eight. The family began with Bloody Marys before lunch, but as Harrison and I were to be driving back to the city immediately following the meal, I chose to enjoy a delicious orange-mint iced tea instead. As the conversation flowed from community issues to travel, world politics, and pop culture, I was impressed by this older generation that held court. I'd never heard my elders speak about anything outside of their own worlds, not to mention England, war, or education.

Elizabeth was intrigued with my knowledge of performing arts and was impressed that I had danced tap, jazz, and ballet. As Harrison and I were saying our goodbyes, I realized that Gran's beautiful dark wide-plank floors were an ideal surface to test my tap. I knew that I could do a shuffle two-step, so I asked Elizabeth if she would like me to tap-dance for her. She was more than delighted! All four elders gave me their rapt attention, and my three minutes of tapping was met with joyful applause. As Harrison and I pulled out of Gran's drive, he said, "It was so nice of you to dance for them. They will remember that forever."

Our drive back to the city was filled with me reminiscing about the wonderful time I'd had with Gran. It was no wonder that Harrison held her in such high regard. In reliving my weekend, I also began to recognize that Gran offered no apologies in letting people know that Harrison was her favorite person. She would, at any moment, tell him how wonderful he was. Their affection was contagious and her loving encouragement was beautiful. Plus, I'd forgotten how super-nervous I was to meet her and realized that I actually had never felt insecure during the visit.

I said, "Harrison, do you think the weekend went well and that Gran liked me?"

He said, without taking his eyes off the road, "There was never any doubt in my mind."

Harrison knew that our stolen weekends would most likely come to a screeching halt once January arrived, so when the opportunity presented itself, we planned a two-day trip

Imagine That!

to Martha's Vineyard. His mother and her sister's family place would be empty for the off season and they welcomed Harrison and his cousins using it. We drove five hours to the coast of Massachusetts and caught a ferry over to the island. We celebrated my first ferry ride out on the deck, as Harrison wrapped his arms around me for warmth.

We arrived late and tired from the travel and I couldn't see much of the place in the darkness. The kitchen and sitting room were one big space, with a fireplace. Harrison made quick use of some cut wood to build a fire, and I prepared a meal of pork chops and vegetables. As the firelight warmed the room, I noticed that there was actually a bed under one of the windows. Since I knew there were bedrooms upstairs, this seemed oddly out of place.

Harrison, anticipating my question, said, "My grandfather, who bought this place when my mom and her sisters were little, often lay there reading, or playing with his grandkids. Even after he died, we never moved it."

We sat on the floor having wine and eating our dinner by the fire. It was so cozy and romantic. At some point, Harrison got onto his grandfather's bed, and I saw him dozing on and off. I placed another log on the fire and was looking around the room at the randomly scattered books when suddenly I felt a gentle presence in the space. And then it was gone.

Both exhausted, we eventually made our way upstairs to bed. When winter's daylight illuminated the room, we woke up and had a simple breakfast. As the house was only a mile from downtown Edgartown, we decided to explore. Very preppie in look, the quaint town hugged the shoreline and offered inviting coffee shops and stores. We continued to the town dock overlooking the marina, and eventually onto the beach, where we walked for hours. That night we even returned to the beach to stargaze and listen to the water lapping the shore. Sitting next to Harrison, wrapped in his arms, I was feeling loved and secure of what we were building. So, I mustered up the nerve to ask him some questions about his past few girlfriends. I first asked, "Why haven't you got some beautiful blonde gracing your arms, and whatever happened to you and your last black girlfriend"? Harrison simply said, "I've dated a few blonde girls before, and they have all been fine, but I've dated them enough to know that look is not what I'm attracted to. As far as my last black girlfriend, she and I were serious for a bit in college, but it just didn't work out. And the break-up was not because we were interracially different." I listened to his answers and did not want to belabor the past, so I leaned in a little more. Harrison turned to me and said, "Right now, you and I are most important." We placed our hands together and made a fist bump and together said, "Solid!"

Imagine That!

The island was actually fairly large, so Harrison and I took slowly paced drives to different towns, occasionally stopping for coffee, muffins, or croissants. The changing townships were apparent, as the style of the houses and landscapes were different from one another. In Edgartown the homes were typically New England style, with white shingles and black or green shutters. When we drove through Oak Bluffs, the homes resembled brightly colored dollhouses. In one area up the island, stones were used to create fencing to divide the properties, while another area had unexpected red cliffs. If just two days in this magical place felt like a relaxing vacation, I could only imagine what the summer months must be like!

Harrison and I returned to the city and the rush of Christmas. I was working a lot, as I knew I had to put aside a few dollars more for the month of January. Retail sales is not a happy environment after Christmas, when the true letdown of the season arrives, and the atmosphere is like a malaise. Freelancers, like myself, tended to get the brunt of the blame if the holiday sales figures were lower than expected, so I wasn't giving my employers any room for criticism. I was working double shifts, stores were busy, and I was taking advantage of my flexible schedule to see Harrison anytime I could. My first Christmas in the city and I WAS IN LOVE! I decided not to fly home to spend Christmas with my family, and since I would not be alone, my mom was in agreement. The season was well into full swing, and I wasn't seeing Eleanor or Christine as much, since they too were in retail, holding managerial positions. The three of us decided to have a "girls' night out" in the New Year when they both returned from visiting their families after the holidays.

One night after work in late December, Harrison and I were having dinner. He said that Gran had called him and invited us to join her for Christmas.

He asked, "Would you like to go?"

I answered, "I would love to join you at Gran's! Let me talk to Nina and see how much time I can manage to take off."

"Come January, and my new job, I don't see how we will be able to spend consecutive days together like we have been," said Harrison.

I had the feeling that Harrison was right. I really wanted this holiday to be special, so I decided to take my boss out for lunch to discuss my holiday schedule. She was a little conflicted in her decision to give me time off – we worked well together, and I was her top sales rep, but she also understood that I was in love, and that Harrison's grandmother had invited me.

"Does the grandmother like you?" asked Nina.

"Yes, she does," I replied. "Listen, I'll work until five on Christmas Eve, and I will come twice before New Year's Eve if you give me the week off."

"Done deal," said Nina.

The excitement leading to Christmas was electric, and I enjoyed gift shopping for Gran, Ethan, Harrison, Mai, Pete, Polly, and his father. I found a beautiful sterling-silver hand mirror, and immediately knew it was the perfect gift for Gran. The other gifts were small and simple, and I got Harrison some cufflinks that he could wear at his new job.

I woke up Christmas Eve excited! I brought my bags to work with me and was ready to go when Harrison picked me up from Bloomingdale's. During the drive, I peppered Harrison with questions about the guest list, schedule of events, and overall program of Christmas at Gran's. Harrison laughed, and then assured me that I would not be disappointed. Little did he know, my expectations would be met by anything not involving prolonged hours on marble flooring wearing high heels. I was exhausted!

As we drove down the long dirt road, the house, beautifully illuminated with warm lights, came into view. Harrison parked the car, grabbed our bags, and as we walked to the door, Gran appeared. Harrison leaned down and kissed her on the cheek. "Merry Christmas, Gran! Thanks for having us!"

She was overjoyed and said, "Merry Christmas to you! I am so thankful you are spending the holiday with me." After hugging us both, Gran continued, "Your room has been prepared, so make yourself comfortable."

I couldn't help but notice the smells permeating the house, and although some were unfamiliar, it reminded me of how my grandmother's house smelled at Thanksgiving.

Gran's dining room had been completely reconfigured into a winter wonderland, the Russian Red Square! The white drapes were pulled tightly closed, and around thirty painted panels (undoubtedly her own artwork), from ceiling to floor, had been placed around the entire room to create a setting that made it seem as if we were right in the middle of Russia! The original dining-room table was surrounded by smaller round tables covered in white tablecloths, glistening silver, blue Spode china, and fresh flowers. A hand-written name card appeared at every seat. The entire thing was so beautiful and so intimate.

I took note of where I was to be seated and who my tablemates would be. It was none other than Harrison's dad, Mike, to my right, and a gentleman I would be meeting for the first time to my left. Harrison informed me that the other gentleman was a family friend, a single man and companion to his mother, Gran's peer. Most

Imagine That!

of the people joining us for dinner were family or close friends who had been in their lives for many years.

I was about to go upstairs and join Harrison in unpacking, but instead wandered into the living room, where stood the biggest tree I had ever seen! And it was real!! The smell of pine was intoxicating, and it was decorated with all sorts of mementos and ornaments. A Florida Christmas this was not!

I grew up putting together a fake tree from a box that was kept in storage. We decorated it with big colorful lights, colorful bulbs, and gold and silver garland. Sometimes my mom would spray white stuff intermittently on the branches so that the tree appeared to have snow on it. We loved that!

Gran's tree seemed so personal; the ornaments she must have collected from her children over the years were unique and meaningful. There were birds, hockey sticks, pinecones, red holly berries, and crafts that the children had hand-made. It was beautiful!

I finally made my way upstairs to the canary-yellow room with the bathtub. Harrison, seeing my wistful glance, valiantly offered to shower in the other room. Guests would not be arriving until after 7:30, and as I ran the water, Harrison returned with a glass of wine.

"You nervous at all about dinner?" asked Harrison.

"Not at all," I said, surprisingly. I loved being with him and his family. I happily floated in my bath as the wine relaxed me.

Harrison dressed conservatively in brown corduroys and a houndstooth blazer, and I wore a red wool jumpsuit with satin lapels. As we headed downstairs, we could hear the voices of the guests arriving and meeting up in the living room.

I was first introduced to Harrison's dad's cousins: Reeve, married with two college-age kids, and John, single and seated at my table. Conversations were of banter between Mike and Beau, compliments of Gran's décor, and Christmas wishes. Salmon appetizers and cocktails were passed around until Gran invited everyone to the dining room. Even for a second time, walking into the dining room was breathtaking! As we were seated, I was introduced to the family friend, and he could not have been more gracious. The food, rack of lamb prepared with fresh herbs and mint sauce, was an unexpected surprise that I really enjoyed. At one point in the evening, we broke out into loud, boisterous Christmas songs that included "We Wish You a Merry Christmas," "O Holy Night," and more. The conversations were lively and interesting, and I soon realized that it was the best Christmas Eve I'd had since being a small child, anticipating the arrival of Santa.

Imagine That!

After dinner, Gran said goodnight to her guests and headed upstairs while a few of the men ventured out onto the porch to enjoy cigars and Sambuca, served with exactly three coffee beans. Taking this as my cue, I made my way upstairs and got cozy in bed to read and think about how magical the night had been.

Christmas morning was relaxing, with a cup of coffee and a light breakfast. Harrison, Gran, Ethan, and I exchanged gifts by the tree. Harrison gave me a simple yet beautiful gold band that had four emerald stones on it. It was pretty and perfect! We all seemed joyful in our exchanges. One of the many gifts that Gran gave Harrison was a handwritten letter. Apparently, this was an annual tradition between the two of them and I could not help but notice how touched he was. Throughout the day, Gran's friends dropped by the house with plants, pies, fruits, chocolates, and other gifts for her. Harrison and I passed the afternoon nibbling on a wheel of Stilton cheese and taking a long walk around the property.

Christmas lunch was scheduled for three at Pete and Mai's house at the top of the road. About fifteen guests gathered in their small, quaint farmhouse, where a huge fireplace and cocktails welcomed us. The atmosphere was festive and intimate, with the smells of turkey and herbs, Russian music playing loudly from the speakers, a beautifully decorated tree, and red-paper-satin-covered windows. The lunch felt like a continued party from the night before, where presents were opened and enjoyed, and interesting conversation and delicious food carried us to 5:30 and, thankfully, naptime! This would be a necessity, as I understood that there was yet another party later that evening, to be hosted by Gran's sister, Elizabeth. A well-established tradition, the annual Christmas Party had been given by their mother from pre-World War II until she died, and Elizabeth had been the hostess to continue the party ever since.

After a long, welcomed nap, Harrison and I wrestled up our energy and joined the party at his great-aunt Elizabeth's. Her home was already packed with guests, beautifully furnished, and also decorated like Gran's. One of her guest rooms was called "the heart room," and every decoration in it was heart-shaped or contained a heart. We enjoyed cocktails, socializing, and mingling among different groups of friends and family. As we made our way through a sea of people, I noticed that the guests were forming themselves into a line. Very curious, I rounded the corner to see Gran and Elizabeth seated at the dining-room table…making ham sandwiches?? These two old ladies, dressed in sparkling gowns and pearls, were serving their guests delicious toasted ham-and-cheese sandwiches and Christmas greetings! It was a perfectly warm and personal way to end the Christmas celebrations. Later that night, lying in bed after the

Imagine That!

festivities, I was reflecting on the holiday with Harrison and his family. I embraced the similarities and welcomed the differences in how we celebrated the holiday.

The remainder of the week was filled with long walks and impromptu lunches and dinners with family, and I traveled back to NYC to work a couple of days before returning to celebrate New Year's Eve. Around twenty of us, Mike and Polly included, dined at Mai and Pete's house with a magnificent meal prepared by Pete and again, I marveled at the table setting, so elegantly styled with gag gifts, party hats, and poppers. Midnight came and everyone broke into singing "Auld Lang Syne." I only knew the first two stanzas and I hummed along to the rest of the lyrics, but I didn't care at all. Caught up in happiness, I presented my first kiss of 1992 to Harrison. I thanked Gran for having me and danced into the New Year reminiscing about the magical holiday.

Chapter 9

As planned, in January, Harrison and Donnie moved into the city and started their new lives in the city. The start of Harrison's new job no longer allowed us the flexibility in seeing one another, which came to a screeching halt, as he often worked long hours, leaving before six a.m. and returning after seven p.m., entertaining clients for dinner. If I worked a late shift, not leaving the store before nine p.m., I would be exhausted by the time I got back to my apartment. Our new normal soon became having to make the most of our Saturdays. Although not seeing him as often, I could see a confidence in Harrison now that he was making money again. I too could save a few dollars. Even though Harrison paid for most of our dinners, I tried every time going Dutch. The times we were able to leave work at a decent hour, we took advantage of our long walks that we so enjoyed together. We would meet at his apartment and decide which direction to walk. Many times finding ourselves in neighborhoods such as Alphabet City, the Village, Chelsea, and SoHo, until one of us was hungry or we just happened to stumble upon a quaint restaurant. My favorite was when we were walking at dusk one evening around his neighborhood and I happened to say, "Let's go to the top of the Empire State Building?"

"Really?" Harrison replied.

"Yes, absolutely." And so we did!

As the months of 1992 flew by, I was auditioning but not landing jobs, and retail sales were slow. For Harrison, however, things were heating up! He loved learning from his coworkers, a great group of guys who took him under their wings. He knew he had to earn their trust and respect, and after mid-year, Harrison was told that he would have to take the Series 7 security exam. As studying became a priority, this further limited our time together. Although it would be an early night for both of us, we planned to go to dinner before his big exam. I sacrificed my lunch hour to get my hair done instead, wanting to look my best for our dinner date. When I arrived at Harrison's apartment around 6:30 p.m., not only did he not notice how dolled up I was, but he was exhausted, and suggested we stay home.

I was immediately reminded of the unwavering commitment black women have to their hair care. Historically, my experience has been watching black women share this painstaking process of getting their hair done. It's an all-day or half-day affair depending on what service you are having done, waiting long hours

– five at a minimum, and it is not uncommon for one to sit for eight hours – sitting in a queue to get washed, conditioned, cut, curled, permed, weaved, braided, pressed, straightened, and then styled. Why we put up with this phenomenon has had me baffled from my first trip to the beauty salon as a little girl. Maybe it's the camaraderie of black women sitting around the beauty salon (a safe place), where we are all as one having similar issues, engaged in conversations that center on kids, church, current events, and personal issues, and that end in lots of gossip and whooping and hollering with laughter. One can go on for hours waiting, so the ladies engage in topics that can keep your mind off the wait.

The suggestion of "staying home" once my hair had been done didn't go over so well with me. It should also be noted that Harrison's older brother had invited him out to Chicago for the weekend, so I already anticipated not seeing him for a few days. As I sat there (looking gorgeous, I might add), he fell asleep! This hair was not going to waste, I decided, so I grabbed my purse and walked down to a local bar that we frequently visited together.

"Hey, Brooke. Where's Harrison?" asked the bartender.

"Well, Jared, I'm alone tonight," I said hotly, swinging myself up on a barstool. Jared nodded, smiled, and introduced me to two young ladies, also neighborhood regulars, sitting a few seats down. The three us began

Imagine That!

chatting and sipping, which progressed to laughing, which ended in me losing track of time and the number of drinks I was consuming. I eventually remembered that I had left Harrison without telling him where I would be, and thanked the girls and wished them goodnight. I began to walk the three blocks back to Harrison's apartment when I was approached and threatened by a homeless man. It was so dark. He was mumbling and motioning with his hands, and I was scared out of my mind. I arrived back at Harrison's place in a panic and found him awake and worried. This was when things went south…

"Brooke! Where were you? Why did you leave? Who brought you back?"

His questions were coming out at a rapid pace and my mind was spinning and I could not focus my thoughts quickly enough to respond. The next thing I knew, I threw up everywhere! All over the floor. All over Harrison. I don't remember what happened next, but I was cleaned and put to bed.

Usually, if I spent the night at Harrison's, he would kiss me goodbye in the mornings, and I would wake up to a nice note from him…Needless to say, that was not the situation when I woke that morning. Instead I was roused by Hillary (*The New Yorker* friend), calling to check in on me.

"Wow, you sound horrible," she blurted.

I quickly summarized what had happened the night before and Hillary started laughing, not at my antics, but in a nervous manner, repeatedly saying, "What have you done?"

She then became serious.

"Oh my goodness, Brooke. You think you guys might break up?"

I said, "I don't know, maybe."

If I were Harrison, I'd break up with me, that was for sure. I couldn't believe that I'd behaved like a spoiled brat the night before his major exam. Hillary and I talked for a while longer before she had to go. I remained in bed, trying to rest before I went back to my apartment or before Harrison came home. I didn't know which would come first, and I was in bad shape. I typically didn't drink, and between feeling sorry for myself and keeping up with the girls, I must have had at least six cocktails.

To my surprise, Harrison came home early, around three p.m. I was still in bed with no energy and looking like a mess.

He walked in, and quietly said, "Hello, how are you feeling?"

I responded as best I could with "Hi, and I'm okay."

He then picked up the phone, called his dad, and informed him that he had passed the test, and that he would be in touch after his weekend in Chicago. I was a horrific person – I felt worse than ever. He hung up

Imagine That!

the phone and started packing. I made a beeline to the bathroom, cleaned up, and upon my return to the room I offered a weak "Congratulations."

Silence from Harrison…

"I'm sorry for my behavior. I was so looking forward to a dinner out with you before your departure this weekend."

His diplomatic response felt like a slap. "I concluded that maybe going out the night before an exam was a bad idea."

Without awaiting my reply, Harrison said, "Let's discuss this when I return from Chicago." And on that abrupt note, he left.

I mustered up all the energy I had and returned to my apartment. Coming home to a few messages on the answering machine was not welcomed but, the one message from Christine got my attention. She was having thoughts of moving back to Illinois. I could not imagine losing Harrison and Christine in the same week. I would call her Sunday night, as I know Saturdays are a big work day for her. I spent the remainder of the evening feeling awful and eventually fell into a fitful sleep. Luckily, I had Saturday off from work, and when I eventually awoke, I found myself reflecting on my selfishness. I completely underestimated the importance of the exam for Harrison. I was reminded of how generous to and supportive of me he always was before auditions…how every single one was my next great opportunity. How had I not given him the same courtesy?

I looked forward to returning to work on Sunday to share this new development with Glenn, as he was always a good sounding board for me. Like Hillary, Glenn began to shake his head and chuckle as I summarized my Thursday-night escapade.

"Why the hell are you laughing? This is serious!" I whined.

He said in a comforting way, "Basically, you chose your hair over supporting Harrison."

"Well…I…"

"You missed an opportunity to show him that what is important to him is important to you."

My throat tightened and my eyes grew watery.

Glenn continued to talk about new relationships and about the "end of the honeymoon phase," when couples become more assertive. I was feeling guiltier by the second.

"Look, I've been around you and Harrison, and I wouldn't think that you two would break up over this, but he might be cautious going forward."

I loved him and realized that losing him would bury me. Being in a relationship required compromise, and when he needed me to be supportive, I'd blown it. The consequences of my behavior could be a life without Harrison. On that dismal thought, I left for lunch.

Imagine That!

When I returned from lunch, Glenn happily told me that Harrison had called! I was filled with mixed emotions. Was he calling to talk or break up with me? I quickly realized that he was too polite to break up with me over the phone, so I went to the storage room to return his call in private. I wanted to let him know that my childish behavior was selfish, and to ask forgiveness, either way.

We spoke our pleasantries and I nervously asked, "When did you return?"

"A few hours ago." Then he asked, "Can I see you for dinner tonight?"

I said yes and immediately delivered my apology. He quickly interrupted, saying that it would be better to talk at dinner instead of on the phone. I begrudgingly agreed, and lived with the uncertainty of our status for the remainder of my shift. Before meeting Harrison, I called Christine, and asked her immediately, "Why are you thinking of moving back to Illinois?" She went into this long monologue about how much she missed her family, especially seeing them during the holidays. Living in Hoboken was nice but the commute to the city was taking its toll on her. Most importantly, her love life was in the dump! She went on to say that during her visit home she reconnected with an old boyfriend and they were starting to communicate more long distance. I couldn't believe what I was hearing. I told her not to make any drastic decisions. I shared with her my recent behavior with Harrison and she too laughed and said, "You both will be fine, Brooke."

Harrison and I met for dinner at one of our favorite restaurants near his place. We hugged and kissed one another and settled into a familiar table. This felt promising, but I was no longer taking anything for granted. Before I could say a word, Harrison started the conversation. "While in Chicago, I was thinking."

I looked into his beautiful blue eyes, melting, and reminded myself to breathe.

"Brooke, I thought about ending this relationship. Your behavior was inconceivable. For hours I was worried about you. I had no idea where you were or if you were in danger, and you finally showed up intoxicated? And left me to handle everything when I had such an important task to prepare for?"

"I'm so, so sorry. Could you accept my apology?" Without making excuses, I began to explain to him why I had behaved so selfishly.

"Look, yes, I forgive you. I don't want to dwell on this any longer. Let's just agree to consult one another on decisions that affect us both."

I nodded enthusiastically. My body was flooded with relief! We were going forward with this relationship! We chatted about Chicago, his brother, and Christine's thoughts on moving back to Illinois. We enjoyed our

Imagine That!

dinner, and then headed back to his place… and right on into bed…where the passion between us was electric.

I had my baby back!

Life returned back to our "new normal," both of us working, and me auditioning. In my freelance world of cosmetics and fragrance, Bergdorf Goodman was becoming my favorite store. It was a beautiful historic building in Midtown that had ambiance of luxury. It was once a private home for the Vanderbilt family. I was booking jobs as an extra on shows like *Law & Order* and *New York Undercover*. I didn't mind the long hours, but the lack of financial gain and recognition were disheartening. I was getting restless.

As months passed by and summer was coming to an end, I realized our first year together was soon approaching! To celebrate, we invited Randy and Hillary to Gran's house for a weekend getaway along with Mike and Polly.

At breakfast that first morning, I turned to Harrison and asked, "What are your thoughts, honey, on being together for a year?"

Smiling, he held up his coffee mug and said, "Keep on drinking!" The four of us burst out laughing and all raised our mugs in agreement. I treasured the milestone. I was so happy in love.

Chapter 10

LATE IN THE FALL, we started a conversation regarding Thanksgiving plans, and since I had not seen my family for quite some time, I was committed to going to Florida. As both Harrison and I were able to arrange some time off, we decided that he would spend Thanksgiving with Gran, and then take a flight out Friday night to join me in Florida for the weekend. I was super excited for my family to meet him, since I had shared so much about him over the phone. My mom was thrilled with the plan, and Nina strangely supportive. Allowing me to avoid Black Friday was a sure sign that she was curious to see if my relationship would survive the visit. She had spoken numerous times on the differences between Harrison's and my family and was fairly convinced that I was just a "phase" that he was going through. Those comments always stung, and as for Harrison's behavior, I never felt any underlying agenda from him. We were loving on each other and it felt great.

Before our visit, however, I did think it necessary to inform Harrison of some of the differences between

Imagine That!

our families so that there were no surprises. My family was a fun-loving, large collection of relatives, usually simultaneously talking, dancing, and eating. Our gatherings were loud and unstructured, and traditions informal…in other words, the exact opposite of his! Harrison never even flinched, and instead told me that he was looking forward to meeting everyone and having a good time.

The week of Thanksgiving, I arrived late on a Wednesday night and got settled with my family to prepare for the best meal of the year. Nobody made dressing (stuffing) the way my grandma prepared it. (I'd asked many times for her recipe, and each time it was given to me differently, with no measurements.) Thanksgiving dinner was usually at my grandparents' house, where, at some point, everyone always ended up.

At any given time on any day, their home was sprinkled with friends and family, adults and kids, passing through to say hello, or to see who else might be around. I personally had always believed that my grandma was the wheel hub to our family's tiny radius of the world – kids making a pit stop after school, aunties retrieving their offspring after work, impromptu social gatherings filling the patio with music and laughter. The front patio performances never disappointed, where my grandparents proudly witnessed their grandchildren school the adults on the latest dance moves. To this day,

I loved to dance, and almost always attempted to join in, despite the family tradition of yelling out, "Sit down, Brooke! You can't dance!" It never prevented me from participation, but instead marked a high point in the gathering.

This particular Thanksgiving, my grandma's home was filled to bursting with the usual suspects. After we stood in a huge circle, holding hands for an uncle's blessing of grace, we feasted on the delicious meal prepared by my grandma, my mom, and her sisters. Much of the discussion that day revolved around Harrison. When was he arriving? What was he like? They would immediately start in on me with their chatter: "Brooke, girrrrl, you look good! New York is really treatin' you right." I had not been home for a year, and I loved seeing them all.

Finally, Friday afternoon arrived, bringing Harrison and cold and cloudy weather, which I had not anticipated. From the airport, we headed directly to my mom's house, where we were warmly welcomed by my mom, Anne, my two brothers, Alexander and Curtis, and my little sister, Kiki. We all got comfortable in the living room with our drinks, and my mom offered Harrison some food, which he declined for the moment. One by one, my extended family stopped by to meet Harrison, and as the parade continued, I lost track of time. I eventually realized that Harrison had not moved, even once, from his chair, due to the continual flow of visitors arriving to meet him.

Imagine That!

It was the first time I ever saw him looking perplexed – he was in need of a break. Normally, Harrison was in complete command of his surroundings, and socially sure of himself; however, my family was in full swing, doing what they did best: visiting, meeting, greeting, and grabbing plates of Thanksgiving leftovers as they came and went.

I squeezed in beside him and asked, "Would you like some food?"

"I'm happy to wait and sit with everyone when you all eat," he replied.

"Well, no one is going to sit all at once, and if you're hungry, then you just grab a plate and eat, and if someone else is hungry at that time, they may join you."

He seemed puzzled at first, and, as he had just left Gran's home, I understood the stark difference. I intervened, became his buffer, and made him a plate of food. While he ate, plate on his lap, more cousins and aunts dropped by to meet him.

The house was filled with loud laughter and multiple conversations all going at once in different directions and overlapping. This unstoppable train went on for hours.

My mom's brothers entered with "Hi, sis! What you got to eat? I heard Brooke's old man came to town."

My aunts would enter with "Hey Anne. Whatcha cooked?"

My mom would answer always with "Go'n get yourself something to eat, and make sure you eat some banana pudding." That was my mom's special dish that all of us enjoyed.

Eventually, the visiting slowed down and Harrison finally got up from the chair. He was exhausted.

My little sister, Kiki, had allowed us to have her room for the weekend and shared my mom's room. The small ranch contained three bedrooms, one bathroom, a living room, and a kitchen – tight quarters for a six-foot-four guy sharing space with his girlfriend's family that he'd just met. He hit the bed immediately and only said, "Wow, you have a large family."

Unfortunately, the next morning, the weather was dreary. At breakfast I made sure to sit with Harrison, and as he ate, he tried to remember some of the names of my family members. I told him not to worry; there was no quiz coming. I had made plans to join some high-school friends to watch the Florida State vs. Florida football game, until two of my cousins from Orlando arrived to meet Harrison. So, to my surprise, he sat right down in the same chair as the night before and the visiting started all over again.

After an hour, I asked my mom to borrow her car so I could take Harrison for a drive. We went for a long drive, seeing some of the sights, and eventually ended up at the T.G.I. Friday's restaurant, seated at the bar. I

Imagine That!

was afraid to ask what he was thinking, but it was an inevitable question. So I asked.

His response was, "I thought I had a large family, but you were not kidding about how large and close your family is. I'm enjoying meeting everyone. But I guess I wasn't prepared to sit for so long! Thanks for the break!"

We had some appetizers and a drink before heading back to my mom's house. As he was leaving first thing in the morning, he wanted to make the most of the remaining trip. As expected, when we returned we were welcomed by many family members ready to talk, dance, eat, and drink. No one held back in telling me to sit down when I was dancing, but of course, that did not stop me from getting in on the fun. Harrison just sat back, relaxed, and joined in on the laughter that was directed at me for not having the greatest of dance moves by their standards. Early Sunday morning, he headed back to NY to prepare for his workweek, while I stayed to join my family at church.

Going to church with my family was one of my favorite things to do when I was home visiting. We still attended the same church I'd grown up going to every Sunday, and it was filled with many of the same families that supported me as a child. In addition to seeing old friends, the singing touched my soul at the core, and the sermon left me wanting to be and become my better self.

As I wrapped up my Thanksgiving visit home, my family told me that they liked Harrison, and were thrilled that I had found love…even if he was white! I couldn't help but wonder how Harrison felt about the all-too-evident differences among our families? I made my way back to NY, and as I was settling back into my apartment, Harrison called. He was surprised that I didn't come to his apartment when I arrived back in the city, but as I was scheduled to work early the next morning, he begrudgingly agreed. While I had him on the phone, I asked, "Well, now that you've survived them, what do you think of my crazy family?"

He was forthcoming. "I enjoyed myself very much in meeting your family. Initially, it was overwhelming, especially because I had just left Gran's house and the setup is different." He said, "I love how they think you can't dance. I find you very sexy when you dance. Does that happen every time you go home, seeing everyone?"

I said, "Yes, pretty much."

"How can your sister, Kiki, focus on doing her homework in the midst of all that noise?"

I said, "It's what we're all used to."

He thought my family was wonderful, and, in a nice kind of way, outspoken. As we continued reminiscing about the trip, I found myself being comforted in knowing that we had survived his visit in meeting my family. I gathered my thoughts and was feeling really good about where Harrison and I stood in our relationship. It truly was solid. We'd adopted this slogan, repeating "solid" while bumping fists at the same time about a year ago when I was feeling insecure about meeting his family. Surpassing another relationship milestone with Harrison felt great.

Harrison continued working hard, learning as much as he could in preparation for opportunity. He liked the smart and talented men surrounding him. They were all family men with a strong work ethic, men with integrity and a willingness to teach him what they knew. Eventually, Don's fortieth birthday party presented an opportunity for me to meet these men, Don, Tom, and Dave, along with their wives and girlfriend. We had dinner at the famous 21 Club, in Manhattan, where I concluded that Harrison was spot on – this group was a sharp, funny bunch of men. They all seemed to want the best for Harrison, and the solidarity among them was genuine.

As for me, I was still in limbo with my acting career. I was taking jobs as an extra, but never getting offers for a steady job. During this time of uncertainty, I was named as one of two actresses under the consideration for a role on a soap opera. Landing this role could mean doing what I loved to do, a steady income, and job security. It took a week of waiting. I so badly wanted the job that I could not sleep, eat, or think. Unfortunately, I did not get it. These were times that left me feeling unworthy. I loved the world of cosmetics and fragrances and enjoyed most of my colleagues, as some of them were actors as well. It was a place of comfort, too, because most of them knew very well that feeling of rejection. Our mantra was, "It's not you personally; it's just that they were looking for something specific."

Argh, how many times had I heard that explanation?

Around the same time, Harrison and Don were deciding not to renew their lease together on their apartment. It made sense; Don's girlfriend and I were staying at their place more often than our own places. The guys' apartment was large enough to accommodate us all, but the men decided in favor of striking out on their own. (I honestly thought that I was a little too vocal in the intimacy department, and that Harrison desired some privacy!)

After my suspenseful week and unfavorable outcome with the acting job, Harrison distracted me with going out to dinner, searching for a new place for him, and discussing the possibility that we move in together.

With the Christmas holiday approaching, Gran invited us again to celebrate Christmas and New Year's with her. I could think of nowhere I'd rather spend the season than surrounded by the magical spirit created by Gran. Before the holidays, Harrison had to find time to look for a new place while I was putting in the long retail holiday hours. With all the hustle that the holiday brought, an unanticipated visit helped us move along in a direction sooner than we expected.

Harrison's dad, Mike, and girlfriend, Polly, were in NYC to see a friend for dinner. They invited us to join them, and although Harrison had work plans, he encouraged me to go. I accepted the invitation and met them at the restaurant on the Upper East Side. During dinner, Mike mentioned that he was preparing to sell his apartment nearby. I politely mentioned to Mike that Harrison was looking to move into his own place after the New Year.

"It certainly would save a lot of time for both of you if you could reach an agreement in either selling or renting your place to him," I suggested. He welcomed that idea and looked forward to speaking to Harrison.

When I joined Harrison later that night and repeated the conversation from dinner, he could not have been more excited about the possibility of his dad's place. I couldn't help but wonder how they had never communicated this information before between them.

Chapter 11

HARRISON AND I RANG IN the New Year of 1993 by taking a leap of faith and moving in together. He had purchased his dad's place on the Upper East Side, a large one-bedroom corner apartment in a six-story pre-war building on Madison Avenue at 94th St. The living room was spacious and had views of both Madison Avenue and 94th St. With both moves complete, we settled in to enjoy our first night together.

Our first morning, we were awakened by a knock on the door. Still undressed, Harrison went to answer and was greeted by an elderly woman named Miriam, who introduced herself as our next-door neighbor, and barged right in and made her way down the hallway to the living room! Meanwhile, I was half naked in the bedroom, door open, clutching the blankets to my chest, and as she introduced herself to me, I confusedly made awkward pleasantries. Her familiarity was astounding – as Harrison stood there in his underwear she continued her monologue by informing us that she had known Mike forever and was happy to serve as our information source regarding anything about the building. And with a quick wave goodbye, she showed herself back down the hall and left!

It didn't take us long to appreciate the location of our shared space, as our new commuter routes to and from work were shortened by almost fifteen minutes. The neighborhood was filled with young families and private schools, and just one block from Fifth Avenue was the entrance to the Central Park Reservoir. On many weekends we would walk the three miles it took to make it around the reservoir, and with museums and restaurants everywhere, we had plenty to see and do. Although the food was great, I personally found many of the restaurants patrons, very conservative. The men wore blue blazers and khakis, while the women wore sweater sets with beautiful diamond earrings – all nice, but I much preferred the downtown feel of NYC, where the music was livelier and the patrons dressed in an eclectic, more fashionable look (i.e. mostly black leather pants and Prada sandals).

More in love than ever, our routine comfortable, we floated through the first six months of the year in our amazing neighbourhood. The cultural diversity surrounding us was rich, and some nights Harrison and I would just walk down Fifth Avenue and appreciate the museums nearby – the Guggenheim, the Metropolitan, and, further down the street, the Frick Museum. The local food market and dry cleaners were family owned and permitted us to have accounts that were payable monthly. As the elderly couples and young families in our building became familiar, we began saying "hello," and our place became a home.

Living together allowed Harrison and me the convenience to grow as a couple. He was working hard, and sometimes that meant he had to entertain clients after work. The perk of living together was that I knew I would see him eventually. Weekends were the best! Saturday mornings we would sleep in late, go to the diner for a meal, then head back to bed for sex and more sleep. I eagerly anticipated our early evening walks, taking in a movie, or meeting friends for dinner. Being in Harrison's presence was super easy, and if we didn't talk, it was okay. Hanging out, doing nothing, sometimes was what we enjoyed the most.

Summer soon approached, and with it, no vacation time in sight for either of us. When possible, we would go to Gran's and spend the weekend in the country. Gran's sister, Elizabeth, had a pool at her house and we used that frequently. As Harrison and I were enjoying the magical development of a solid love between us, many of our friends were also planning their futures and getting engaged. Time was moving quickly, as days turned into months, seasons coming and going, and Autumn arousing excitement for what was to come, as the beautiful leaves fell. We found ourselves again planning for the holidays. Our third Thanksgiving celebration together was dined at Elizabeth's house, where the home was filled with thirty guests of family and friends, feasting on amazing food, laughter to beat the band and a welcomed weekend of relaxation. Christmas brought on a whole new excitement. It would be my first time experiencing a real Christmas tree of my own. We spent an afternoon shopping for the perfect tree and its trimmings. Once bought and placed in the right spot of the apartment, it was ready for decorating. It permeated the smell of pine throughout the apartment well into the hallway. Harrison knew of my excitement of a real tree, so he left me in my glory of decorating. He enjoyed the evening in sharing my excitement with a couple of beers and watching T.V. The night fell, and as I was finishing the trimmings, I noticed snow falling ever so lightly. The look I gave Harrison was "we have to go outside." Not too much convincing and no destination in mind, we found ourselves walking on Fifth Avenue. Holding hands and not a person in sight, we started to joyfully sing Christmas songs. The snow continued to come down as we found ourselves ten blocks south, standing on the steps of the Metropolitan Museum. I stood a few steps above him to look into his beautiful blue eyes and planted a kiss on his lips. I couldn't believe the solitude that surrounded us as we made our way back to the toasty apartment. Harrison knew all too well that I was in the Christmas spirit, and in no rush for bed. He and I curled up near the beautifully decorated tree and lost ourselves in each other's arms.

Making our first Christmas debut of a joint Christmas card of Harrison and me, I was all too ready to share with family and friends. One afternoon, I came home from work and was opening the daily delivery of holiday cards. We were receiving so many that I began to hang them as festive decorations in the apartment. I opened one from his mother, not realizing until later that it had been addressed to Harrison only. Although it was a holiday card, the letter included a description of her recent travel to Brazil, and, as I read on, a detailed account of the beautiful women from that country, and her suggestion on him taking a visit there. Without warning, I suddenly felt that old insecurity creeping back to claim me.

When Harrison arrived home, he easily explained away her oversight, and even went as far as addressing the situation with his mother directly by asking her to be more sensitive with her content on other women in future correspondence. I was grateful to him for understanding my feelings, but felt that maybe his mom did not approve of me? I knew, in my heart, that it was not her intention to upset me (or Harrison, for that matter), but I allowed my lack of education to resume its

Imagine That!

familiar, shameful place back inside. It occurred to me that a secure woman would never think twice about the card other than to marvel at the amazing opportunity in visiting such a beautiful place...

We enjoyed going to Gran's for a magical Christmas Eve, where we were showered with her regal yet inviting warmth, and decided to spend New Year's Eve with Randy and Hillary in Westchester, a county north of Manhattan. We celebrated the ball dropping like an old-school house party with good friends, music, food, wine, and beer.

As memorable as that holiday was, Harrison and I were entering 1994 with our second year of living together. Christina's move back to Illinois left me with sadness but hopeful for her future. I knew there were some hard questions that I soon had to answer for myself.

I started working more and auditioning less. We started spending more time with other couples, going to sports events such as Rangers' games, escaping to East Hampton for weekends, and taking long drives north to Harrison's and Donnie's alma mater, Williams College. Weddings were now in our cycle of weekends, and the more time I spent with Harrison's friends, the more I realized that I was actually envious (but not resentful) of their camaraderie, their cleverness, and their knowledge base. These friendships I witnessed were undeniably priceless. They were all "best versions" of themselves.

I wanted to read more, learn, study – whatever it took to achieve my best self. It was time for me to make a decision: Was I going to get my ass in gear and become a real, full-time, gainfully employed actress? Or was I going back to school? Being around Harrison and his friends motivated me, and as an adult, I alone was responsible for giving myself what I didn't have growing up. I wasn't sure how Harrison would feel about me going back to school, but it became an option that I had to examine. I was ready and confident that getting my bachelor's degree would free me of my insecurities, and potentially open up more doors. Was it possible that this new direction might mean the end of Harrison and me?

At work, I started to share my concerns with Glenn. He was very supportive and encouraging and reminded me that Harrison loved me. Nina, however, saw things differently. It was not often that we had scheduled shifts together, but one day we did, and were even able to take a lunch break together. We walked to a local restaurant, where we ordered the rosemary roasted-chicken salads and began chatting about the usual retail business rubbish, like which companies were hiring, which booking promotional sales, etc., when the conversation took a surprising turn. It would be the starting point of many similar conversations.

"So, how are you and Harrison doing?"

"Amazingly well," I responded, listing some of the fun things we were doing together and saying that living with him was surprisingly easy.

"How long has it been now? At least three years, right? Have you thought about the long term with him?" she continued.

I wasn't prepared for these questions. Harrison and I were going in a positive direction, and I felt confused as to why she was doubtful of what we had. I certainly was not taking our relationship for granted, but never did I think Harrison gave me reason to think otherwise.

I struggled to keep the conversation light. "He is working very hard at his business while I still pursue acting."

She tried to reroute the conversation by complimenting me. "Brooke, you are a fine black woman, well-spoken and beautiful. As your friend, I'm here to tell you that Harrison will never marry you. As long as she is alive, his grandmother will never allow it."

I felt emotionally punched, the air in my chest gone. Not knowing what to say, I responded as best I could. "Right now, we're just navigating careers and figuring it out."

Lunch ended, awkwardly...and when I returned to work, I shared the conversation with Glenn.

"Unfortunately, Brooke, Nina doesn't know Harrison, and she has not heard you describe your time with his grandmother," he pointed out.

I knew he was right but I had to admit it; her comments hurt! I couldn't put into words how utterly deflated I felt. I eventually decided to listen to Glenn and forget the unpleasant lunch with Nina. I was in a healthy relationship with someone who loved and respected me, right?

After that day, whenever we worked together, she began the conversation anew, even including others, and petitioning their two cents in asking if Harrison and I would ever marry. The group's examination of my personal life started to get in the way of my performance at work; I wasn't amused by my coworkers, since the topic of downtime conversation was always Harrison and me. I wanted to avoid the noise in my head about marriage and stay focused on what I needed to do for self-improvement. The opportunity presented itself; I started booking more hours at Bergdorf Goodman and Saks Fifth Avenue, thereby avoiding the discord between Nina and me.

Sadly, I had always admired her amazing work ethic and I missed Glenn, terribly.

Months passed, memories were made, and Harrison and I were very happy. One weekend, Harrison's mom invited us to visit her in Saratoga Springs. The five-hour ride was beautiful and we enjoyed a Saturday picnic on Saratoga Lake, taking turns navigating the boat across the glistening water.

Somehow, our conversation turned to education, low-income families, single-parent homes, and crowed public schools. I actually found myself speaking on these all-too-familiar subjects without feeling regret or personal embarrassment. Having been raised by a single mom earning a low income, I knew that her most pressing concerns were paying for food and rent. I don't think my mom ever mentioned a private school or college to my siblings or me. She expected us to earn our high-school diplomas, and after graduation, get jobs. My entire family attended the same community school, and it was a huge part of my social life. The school spirit was amazing, and only looking back did I realize that I was never instructed on how to study, achieve good grades, or think beyond a high-school education.

My senior year of high school, I'd attended a thespian conference where colleges were looking to recruit talent. Miami University offered to give me a scholarship, but I never pursued it because I had no idea how to go about accepting such a gift, nor did I have the guidance necessary to make it happen. The longer I spoke to Harrison's mom, the more I felt the need to get my BA, as I now had the ability to find out the answers for myself. And if, for some reason, along the way I got a job in acting, it would only enrich my future.

One of the highlights of the weekend was talking to Harrison's stepdad. He was by far one of the most interesting people I'd ever met. His life's work with the civil-rights movement was one of inspiration. He further inspired me to reach my potential by sharing his civil-rights stories and withholding no judgments. He was able to turn any location or moment into a classroom, and I was a willing student in his presence. On that day, he made me feel that anything was possible.

Chapter 12

AFTER THAT WEEKEND AWAY, I felt that I had finally connected with Harrison's mom. I started to envision my own five-year plan, and once I felt fairly confident in my path, I knew it was time to approach Harrison with my new declaration. Although I knew he sensed that I was at a crossroad, I was not sure exactly how our relationship would look once my plan was revealed.

Early in the week we met at one of our favorite local restaurants to have dinner. We arrived at the restaurant and found two spots at the bar, where we typically liked to eat, as it always felt so relaxed. The bartender took our orders and then, as we faced one another, I realized: now or never, it was time to share.

I began by saying to Harrison, "There is something that I have been thinking about for quite some time and I want to talk to you about it."

"I'm all ears," he replied.

"Losing out on the soap-opera job left me defeated and uninspired. I was thinking of going back to school to get my BA degree."

"I noticed you haven't been auditioning much. Have you lost your passion for acting?" asked Harrison.

"I don't know anymore. Considering the training I had, I imagined that by now I would have a full-time acting job."

After high school, as many of my friends were going off to college, I'd auditioned for and was accepted into an acting school in NYC called the American Academy of Dramatic Arts, known nationally as a highly reputable acting school. I was thrilled to be joining the amazing and talented teachers and students who'd graduated from there (like Robert Redford). Unfortunately, I ran out of money, could no longer afford the tuition, and was not asked to return. My mother was not experienced with this sort of matter – she could not support me in getting a loan or financial aid. Devastated as I was, I did not move back home, but stayed on the East Coast and lived with a great-aunt and -uncle, which they allowed me to do until I could figure out my next move.

Incredibly, the American Musical Dramatic Academy eventually contacted me by phone within four months and encouraged me to audition and enroll. I told the woman on the phone that, although I was thrilled to be invited to audition, I had no way of paying for the two-year program if I was accepted. She kindly informed me that I qualified for financial aid. What? They would pay for me to attend? I was beyond excited! I confirmed an audition date and with my acceptance letter secured financial assistance. I completed the two-year program, graduating with a degree in musical theater. As I prepared for graduation, I auditioned for a student film called *The Tibetan Method*. I got the job and the film actually aired on TV! That experience was amazing, but it left me with inflated false hope. I wrongly assumed that by graduating and having this student film under my belt, more jobs would follow.

As I poured out my heartfelt desire to go back to school, Harrison listened carefully, and then replied, "If this is what you want, I'm here to support you in any way I can." He continued by asking, "What schools do you have in mind?"

"I have not even begun to look," I admitted. "I was not sure you would support this decision."

He said, "I love you and I want to see you happy."

Without delay, I started researching schools. A friend suggested that I take a look at the New School for Social Research. She said it seemed like a good fit for someone like me: a slightly older, more serious student, committed to reaching my educational goals. Upon attending open house nights at a few schools in Manhattan, I discovered that she was right. The New School for Social Research seemed a perfect fit. I met with the director of admissions, submitted my credentials, and was accepted. They even gave me credit for attending AMDA!

From that moment, my confidence skyrocketed! I was working on something for myself that I'd never imagined possible. I continued to work freelance jobs and became an assistant to some of my professors to help offset the cost of my continuing education. Despite all of this, there were many times when I was short with tuition fees, which Harrison gladly volunteered to help with. I was learning so much and I was surrounded by students committed to getting the most out of their studies. Some of them owned their own businesses and each brought their life experience into the classroom. We all wanted to be there, fully engaged, discussing history, social issues, art, philosophy, and much more. I enjoyed every bit of the process, taking field trips at night to the Metropolitan Museum, joining study groups. I became a thinker and unlocked tools I never even knew I had.

Going back to school and working full time left me busier than ever, and at the same time, Harrison was just as busy. In a remarkably short time, he's learn enough from his colleagues Tom, Dave and Capelin that it was paying off for him financially. We were both performing at our best and loved sharing our newly honed skills – my knowledge of school subjects and his of expensive wine, earned while sipping with clients! We both seemed like we were growing and evolving.

My desire to avoid working with my boss was still a nettlesome presence in my life. The more confident I

Imagine That!

became, the more pressure I received from Nina about not being married. Eventually, I allowed her to get the best of me – could what she was saying be possible? Would I never actually get a commitment from Harrison?

That day I came home from work feeling down and could not shake my fears. When Harrison asked, "What's wrong?" I sat down on the couch and uncontrollably started to cry through an explanation of my doubts. He quietly listened to me as I recounted the happenings over the last few months at work and how our relationship was the topic of conversation. I gave him the unedited summary of the majority vote: Harrison would never commit to Brooke.

Harrison gathered his thoughts and calmed me down. As ever, he was sure of himself, and in that moment he could not have been clearer. "I'm very sorry that you have been experiencing this nonsense at work. I wish you would've told me sooner and not gone through this alone. We are solid, Brooke! None of those people know me, nor do they know my intentions. If you ever want to discuss marriage or commitment, please never hesitate to talk to me. I love you and will always give you the truth."

I confessed through my sniffles, "In the beginning, when my boss would start the conversation about us, I was shocked and tried to ignore her. But now that we have been together for quite some time, she is beginning to say things that I now think may hold some truth, and

I'm scared. I love you, Harrison, and I can't possibly see my life without you."

He said, "I believe in the commitment of marriage, but because my parents and your parents are both divorced, I want to approach marriage differently. Yes, I see myself with you, in marriage, but right now, I cannot afford a family."

"What do you mean?" I asked.

"With marriage, I assume you will want kids, and I cannot afford to support us in the manner I want to right now." He continued by sharing the goals he had for himself financially (a million dollars before he proposed) and described how he saw himself as a husband. He said, "I love you, but I am not ready for marriage right now." I listened and understood, but the tears continued to roll down my face.

Many times throughout our relationship, Harrison and I had had important conversations, and they were conducted rationally. This night ended with me crying softly from the comfort of his strong arms. Intellectually, Harrison was right, but hearing that he was not ready to marry me was excruciating.

Our lovemaking that night was so passionate. We were expressing so much through touch – me saying, "I don't want to lose you" and he, "I'm never letting you go." It was beautiful and the release from us both was matched intensely.

Imagine That!

I actually called my mother the next day and gave her the abbreviated version of what was happening at work. Her response was classic Mom. She said, "Well, what will make you happy? Being with Harrison in love, or leaving him because he is not ready for marriage?"

I quickly answered, "Being with him, of course!"

She continued, "Stop listening to folks who have no business in your relationship. And if you and Harrison don't make it down the aisle, well, you've had a beautiful time with him."

Harrison and I managed that hurdle really well, and from time to time, he would ask if my coworkers were harassing me about not being married. I assured him that they were, but their comments no longer bothered me. Something in me had changed. I became more and more confident, and the new armor of attending school helped to protect my feelings. My constant insecurity disappeared, and I was in a good place with myself – with a new attitude and limitless possibilities!

For a long time, I'd been plagued by "not knowing" the answers to questions. I was embarrassed; I felt stupid or judged. Now, when asked a question about something unfamiliar, I felt quite content admitting, "I don't know." Harrison also noticed my increasing self-worth and loved every bit of it!

Most of our circle of friends and family were finding success in their lives. So it was not surprising when, one evening, we received a phone call from Celine, announcing her engagement. She had been dating this guy, Dylan, for a little over two years. They were planning on getting married later in the year. Both Harrison and I expressed our congratulations and support. Celine continued, "Brooke, you have become one of my good friends, and I would be more than honored if you would be one of my bridesmaids?"

I said, "I'm honored! Of course I will!" It was humbling to know that she wanted me to be in her wedding. She and Dylan decided to have a fall wedding on Martha's Vineyard, in the same church where her parents married, long ago, and the reception was held on the property of their family home. Celine was a beautiful bride, wearing a long ivory wedding dress accessorized with generations of lace crowning her head. It was a perfect September day with beautiful blue skies, and a well-attended wedding with loads of their family and friends. When the bandleader announced the tossing of the bride's bouquet, the single women shrieked with laughter and congratulations as it fell right into my hands!

As the excitement wore down, Harrison's mom came over to me and invited me to take a walk with her. I accepted, and we walked away from the huge tent where the guests were continuing their dancing and fun.

Imagine That!

She said, "I think it's time that you meet my mom and dad." I was initially confused, for I had been told that her parents had passed years ago. We slowly approached a massive red maple tree that separated the main house from the barn on their property. We stood in front of the tree, our arms interlocked, and she started speaking.

"Mom, Dad, I want you to meet Brooke, a lovely and special person that Harrison has brought into our lives. And I know that if you were here, you both would adore her, as we all do."

As I realized the significance of where we were standing, tears sprang from my eyes and rolled down my cheeks. She turned to me and said, "Brooke, meet my parents. They are here in spirit, buried under this tree, which provides us with so much beauty and strength every time we are in its presence."

I turned to face her, gave her a hug, and said, "Thank you so much for bringing me here and for sharing your parents."

By this time, Harrison and some cousins had ventured down to the tree to join us. From that moment on, I felt accepted by his mom, and, without any doubt, loved by her. There were no guarantees that Harrison and I would marry, but I no longer harbored insecurities. Celine and Dylan's wedding was more than fun for me. It was validation.

Chapter 13

(1997)

HARRISON AND I CONTINUED to repeat the work/school cycle, sharing financial gains and educational goals along the way. Our life was busy but carefree, until one Sunday in April. As I lay in our bed soaking in the afterglow of lovemaking, I realized that I was late in getting my period…yeah…two days late. As we were getting dressed for brunch, I mentioned this little irregularity to Harrison.

"Well…I'm sure this happens all the time," he said.

"Not to me," I replied.

As the mood in the room quickly changed, the air became tense and thick. Harrison lamely insinuated that, somehow, I might have intentionally allowed myself to become pregnant. What the fuck was he saying?? Did he think I was trying to trap him? I was devastated.

Unsuccessfully trying to gain control, I got loud. "REALLY? In no uncertain terms I can tell you that I do not want a baby now! And if you honestly think that, then you have no idea who I am!"

We ate brunch in silence and retreated to our corners afterward. I decided to take a walk around the reservoir while Harrison headed back to the apartment to finish some reading for work. As I circled the park, my mind was racing. How could I convey to Harrison, in a non-blaming way, what I was thinking? I decided that I would just start with what I knew best. Me.

I came back and approached him confidently. "Listen, Harrison. I saw my mom raise four kids alone, struggling every minute of every hour of the day to make ends meet. There is no way I'd want a baby without a husband. Perhaps we are allowing the situation to get the best of us, but I too have goals for myself, or maybe you were not listening? I know you are not ready to be a father; I just want your support in the hard decisions I may have to prepare for if I am pregnant."

He listened and quietly said, "Let us not have that discussion or make that decision until we are sure."

That night was a long one, with very few words between us. He went to work early the next morning, and as I had class later that day, I was home alone for several hours. By late morning, I got my period! I called him immediately at work and told him the news. He sounded relieved, and, at the same time, very guilty for his earlier conduct.

We mustered up light conversation at dinner, and I gingerly reiterated my love for him, and my desire to only have children with a man who wanted them with me. Until this point, I'd never profoundly felt the weight my mother carried – in and out of the court system fighting for child support. I would never use pregnancy as a means to keep a man bound to me.

He apologized and said, "I know that, but I panicked. Will you forgive me?" Of course I forgave him, and we managed our way through reconciliation. I was preparing for graduation and living my life now with a determined purposed, and Harrison was making a sizable amount of money that would give him the financial freedom he sought. We were simultaneously in this space of liberation, and I felt proud for us both.

Interestingly, this revelation brought about a fear. While my mental strength was at an all-time high, I realized that I was in a vulnerable position – emotionally and financially. I loved Harrison so much and being with him forever would be a dream come true, but I knew that if we were "not to be," I was strong enough to survive. Was Harrison feeling the same way? Under no circumstances did I want to believe that committing to me was his only option. A break-up would hurt like hell, but I knew I could endure and move on, successfully.

I decided to have lunch with Glenn to sort through my thoughts regarding where I believed my relationship with Harrison could be heading. He, too, agreed that if Harrison and I split, I could survive the break-up. Glenn also assured me a safe spot to land at his place for three months, if I needed it. I had some cash that would allow me first and last month's rent, but living in NY you needed a bit more cushion than that.

I was thrilled to hear that my mom and sister were traveling to see me march and receive my diploma! Since my family was coming, Gran and Ethan kindly offered to plan a graduation lunch for me at the Yale Club. Busy with invites from a few friends and family, I was conflicted. Harrison's work schedule was crazy, and unfortunately, he would not be able to attend either the ceremony or the lunch. I was surprisingly fine with his absence, as this accomplishment was all mine, and it didn't matter to me if I stood alone.

Harrison and I unexpectedly went to a casual event in Williamstown, which was well attended by most of his friends, and despite the fact that I barely saw him as he caught up socializing with his best buds, I had a wonderful time mingling and socializing on my own. Armed with the knowledge of my impending degree, my insecurities no longer accompanied me…and completely vanished. Instead of envy, I felt only unity. Others noticed my self-esteem as well, especially Harrison's and now my best friend too, Donnie A!

"Brooke, you're glowing and are radiating self-satisfaction! What's going on?" said Don.

Despite my instinct to tell him about my vanishing insecurities while on the Williams campus, I responded, "I feel great!"

The next few weeks were a grind for both Harrison and me. He barely came home at night, which I interpreted as dinner with clients. As I had two final papers I was working on, Harrison asked if I'd like to go to Martha's Vineyard for the weekend.

"It would be quiet and no distractions," he promised. I wasn't quite sure about going, but I eventually warmed up to the idea of solitude for study and work. That Friday night we drove north, and four hours later, were enjoying a late dinner with Harrison's cousin, Chris. He was fresh out of medical school, and was also at the family home, soaking up the off-season quiet.

Saturday morning we woke up early to coffee and a light breakfast. Harrison and Chris knew I wanted to get started on my papers, so they vanished after breakfast to go into town. The weather was overcast so it made it easier for me to work all morning and well into lunch. When Harrison and Chris returned, I was more than ready for a break.

"Would you like to go for a walk? Stretch your legs?" asked Harrison.

Imagine That!

"Absolutely," I replied. "Chris, will you join us?"

"Chris is going to work on some medical stuff," interjected Harrison before Chris could even answer.

"Umm, I'm speaking to Chris, Harrison. Chris, please join us?" I tried again.

Chris confirmed what Harrison had indicated, even more adamant in his response. As Harrison and I walked away from the house, I made my opinion known immediately. "How can you be rude to Chris and not include him?"

He didn't say a word. We walked quietly toward town.

After we had walked about a mile, we came upon the Nature Trail. Harrison and I agreed to continue on – Lord knew I needed the calming embrace of serenity present on the wooded trail. The symphony of the birds was a treat, and the lack of conversation was beginning to calm me. Eventually, the trees opened, revealing a two-person bench with an amazing view of the water.

Harrison asked, "Would you like to sit?"

"Sure," I replied.

It was so beautiful, and there was not a soul in sight as we sat there gazing out at the water. Eventually, Harrison broke the silence.

"Brooke, you mean a lot to me, like my family, and I love you."

I looked at him and said, "I love you, too."

At that moment he stood up, got down on one knee, produced a red box with the most beautifully sparkly ring, and asked, "Will you marry me?"

OMG! OMG! OMG! I stood up, and as I paced back and forth, I shouted, "YES!!"

He picked me up and we were both saying, "I love you! I love you!" over and over again!

I don't remember much after that, other than a long, lanky kid walking by afterward with a look on his face like, "What did I just come upon?" I do, however, remember Harrison explaining on our walk back his last few weeks of absence – he was not at home most nights because he was visiting the jeweler to become educated on stones, clarity, and color. He also mentioned that Donnie came to him in Williamstown and said, "Dude, you are losing Brooke, and that is a big mistake. He assured Donnie that he was ready to ask me to marry him, but was waiting on the right time. "I want to love you forever, Brooke," said Harrison.

Through happy tears of joy, I echoed his desires. I confessed that for the previous few weeks I had been unsure of where we were going with our future.

"I only wanted pure happiness for you, Harrison, and I was ready to let you go. But you are choosing me to be your wife, and I will forever make sure that you're happy."

Imagine That!

Hand in hand, we walked the trail back on cloud nine. I congratulated him on a job well with the ring, a 2.5-carat round-cut diamond, brilliant in color, set in platinum. Never could I have imagined that something so beautiful would rest on my finger! As we approached the house, there was Chris. He was sitting on the lawn, playing the guitar while waiting for us to return, as he knew all along of the life changing event that had just taken place for Harrison and me.

Imagine that!

On a warm summer night, twenty-five years ago, there was a mutual attraction between two very different individuals that led to a special connection. They managed through disappointments and success, loving each other desperately, and building a bond that transcended racial barriers. It didn't matter to Brooke that Harrison was in debt, and it didn't matter to Harrison that Brooke didn't have a college degree. What mattered most was their respect and love for each other.

Harrison is a man of strength, integrity, loyalty, and truth. With our hearts, communication, and courage, and against all odds, we have loved one another more ways than one can imagine!

Imagine that!

CPSIA information can be obtained
at www.ICGtesting.com
Printed in the USA
LVHW021546080523
746420LV00012B/112/J